Feminine Positive Affirmations for Black Women:

Become Divine Women and Live a Life in Abundance and Joy. Increase Self-Love, Wealth, Success and Self-Esteem Forever.

Sacred Sound Healing

Contents

INTRODUCTION

CHAPTER ONE 1

Beyond The Surface 1

RELIGION AND SPIRITUALITY.............................. 4

EMOTIONAL HEALTH AND SPIRITUALITY 11

IMPACTS OF SPIRITUALITY ON MENTAL
HEALTH 13

IMPROVING SPIRITUAL HEALTH 16

AFFIRMATIONS FOR SPIRITUALITY 18

KEY POINTS...21

CHAPTER TWO... 22

SELF AWARENESS..22

WHY DO I NEED TO KNOW MYSELF?...................27

Self-Love 28

Independence 29

Clear Decision Making... 30

LEARNING ABOUT YOURSELF 33

Be Still 34

Distinguish Between Who You Are And Who You
Want To Be 35

Find Out Your Strengths And Weaknesses............. 36

Follow Your Passion 38

AFFIRMATIONS FOR SELF AWARENESS 39

KEY POINTS 41

CHAPTER THREE **43**

SEXUALITY 43

Female Sexual Problems 47

Causes Of Female Sexual Problems 48

Diagnosis Of Female Sexual Problems 50

Prevention Of Female Sexual Problems 55

LIVING ABOVE THE STIGMA OF STDS 56

Honesty Is Key 56

Importance of Breaking The Stigma 59

Affirmations For A Positive Sexual Health 60

Key Points 63

CHAPTER FOUR **65**

WORKPLACE 65

Home Office..67

Farm or Outdoor Location 68

Store 69

PURPOSE OF THE WORKPLACE 69

WORKPLACE STRUGGLES 72

Sexual Harassment 74

Kiss up, Kick down 76

Gender Inequality 77

The Toxic Workplace 79

Fatigue and Ill Health...81

Lack of Enthusiasm 82

Low Turnover Rate 82

Stifled Growth... 82

COPING WITH WORKPLACE TOXICITY 83

Find Support.. 83

Stay Positive.. 84

Take a Break.. 85

Meditate 85

Surround Yourself With Positivity 86

Quit 86

AFFIRMATIONS 87

KEY POINTS.. 89

CHAPTER FIVE.. 90

FRIENDSHIPS.. 90

WHAT ARE FRIENDSHIPS? 92

FORMS OF FRIENDSHIPS....................................... 95

So What Does He Say?.. 96

Friendships Of Utility 96

Friendship of Pleasure.. 100

Friendships Of The Good 101

QUALITIES OF A FRIEND 105

Loyalty..105

Trust Worthiness 106

Acceptance 107

Listening Ears 108

Reciprocity 108

AFFIRMATIONS 111

KEY POINTS.. 113

CHAPTER SIX 114

FINANCES... 114

PERSONAL FINANCES 117

Essence of Personal Finances...................117

Meeting Money Needs............................ 119

Managing Your Income 120

Budgeting, Spending, Saving, and Investing 121

Having the Family Financially Secured 123

Keeping Off Bad Debts 124

Improving the Standard of Living........... 125

RULES OF PERSONAL FINANCE 126

Have a Goal... 127

Start Saving Early 127

Distinguish Wants From Needs 128

Differentiate between Assets and Liabilities..........128

Live Within Your Means...........................129

Don't Invest in Anything You Don't Understand...130

Settle Debts With the Highest Interest Rate First . 131

Prepare for Emergencies 131

Educate Yourself 132

AFFIRMATIONS 133

CHAPTER SEVEN 137

THE CAREER WOMAN 137

A JOB AND A CAREER 141

Requirements 143

Time 143

Income 147

CAREER DEVELOPMENT 147

THE STAGES OF CAREER DEVELOPMENT 148

Self-Assessment 148

Career Awareness 149

Goal-Setting 150

Skill Training 151

Performing 151

FACTORS INFLUENCING CAREER
DEVELOPMENT 152

Personal Characteristics 152

Physical and Mental Abilities 152

Socio-Economic Factors 153

Chance Factors 153

IMPROVING YOUR CAREER DEVELOPMENT .. 154

Learn Everyday 155

Be Indispensable 155

Interaction 156

Figure out your Weaknesses 156

Be Yourself, Always 157

POSITIVE CAREER AFFIRMATIONS 157

KEY POINTS.. 160

CHAPTER EIGHT.. **161**

THE WOMAN LEADER....................................... 161

WHO IS A LEADER?.. 162

QUALITIES OF A LEADER 163

A Sense of Purpose 163

Empathy... 164

Vision 165

Creativity.. 166

Motivation 167

Making Room for Improvement 168

Communication 169

LEADERSHIP MISCONCEPTIONS 170

WOMEN IN LEADERSHIP................................. 172

Value for Balance.. 173

They are More Empathetic................................ 174

Great Multitaskers... 174

Better Communicators 175

Flexibility 176

Inclusiveness..176

Emotional Intelligence 177

Ability to Handle Crises...178

Defying the Odds 178

POSITIVE AFFIRMATIONS FOR LEADERSHIP .179

KEY POINTS..181

CHAPTER NINE **182**

THE BLACK WOMAN AND BEAUTY 183

BEAUTY..185

General Overview of Beauty 185

BEAUTY; THE INSECURITY................................186

Low Self-Esteem 189

Overthinking. 190

Self-Condemnation.. 191

Self-Isolation..192

Desperation..193

Exercise Daily 194

Skin and Haircare, Manicure, and Pedicure..........195

Go Shopping 196

Keep Records 197

Share with Others 198

Black Beauty 199

POSITIVE AFFIRMATIONS FOR BEAUTY 203

KEY POINTS.. 205

CHAPTER TEN.. **206**

A HEALTHY MIND.................................... 206

THE MIND IS DISSECTED 209

TAKING CONTROL 216

Acceptance... 219

Switch POVs 220

Positivity Always! 222

POSITIVE AFFIRMATIONS FOR A HEALTHY
MIND 224

KEY POINTS.. 226

CHAPTER ELEVEN **227**

BLACK WOMEN ENTREPRENEURS...................227

WHO IS AN ENTREPRENEUR? 228

GISELLE KNOWLES-CARTER 229

LYNDA RAE RESNICK 231

OPRAH WINFREY 232

MADAME C.J WALKER 233

DANA ELAINE OWENS 234

SMALL
BUSINESSES..236

SCALABLE STARTUPS......................................236

SOCIAL ENTREPRENEURSHIP......................... 238

WHAT DOES IT TAKE TO BE AN
ENTREPRENEUR? 239

KNOWLEDGE 241

RISK-TAKING 242

PLANNING 243

PROFESSIONALISM 244

AFFIRMATIONS 246

KEY POINTS 248

CHAPTER TWELVE **249**

SELF-LOVE 249

WHAT IS SELF-LOVE? .... 252_Toc111570722

SELF-LOVE VS NARCISSISM 255

PERFECTIONISM AND ILLS 257

The Ills of Perfectionism..........................257

DEALING WITH PERFECTIONISM 259

WHY PRACTICE SELF-LOVE?............................ 262

HOW DO YOU PRACTICE SELF-LOVE? 263

Quit The Comparisons 263

Be Around People You Feel Good With 264

Make Room for Healthy Habits 267

AFFIRMATIONS 269

KEY POINTS 270

CHAPTER THIRTEEN ....258..**272**

MENTAL/EMOTIONAL HEALING 272

WHAT IS EMOTIONAL HEALING? 273

WHY EMOTIONAL HEALING? 274

EFFECTS OF EMOTIONAL PAIN 275

Anger..276

Low Self-Esteem 277

Insomnia...278

STAGES OF HEALING 280

STAGE ONE: GRIEF AND DENIAL......................281

STAGE TWO: ANGER..282

STAGE FOUR: DEPRESSION 284

STAGE FIVE: ACCEPTANCE................................286

POSITIVE AFFIRMATIONS FOR MENTAL
HEALING 287

KEY POINTS..290

CHAPTER FOURTEEN............................ 291

YOU ARE ENOUGH...291

WHAT IS SELF-WORTH? 294

Confident Approach to Solving Problems.............295

Realistic Expectations 296

Have Healthier Relationships 297

Resilience...298

HOW TO IMPROVE YOUR SELF-WORTH......... 300

Come to Terms with the Positives.........................302

Do What You Love..303

Address Yourself With Care 305

POSITIVE AFFIRMATIONS 307

KEY POINTS..309

Conclusion **310**

Introduction

Dear black woman, I see you and all your work to ensure that things work out for you. I see your tears, tenacity, and drive for nothing but the exceptional. That is why I am writing this book of affirmations to encourage you.

This book contains affirmations for every stage and season. I poured myself into writing this book for you. I hope you enjoy it!

CHAPTER ONE

Beyond The Surface

"Get in touch with the depth and silence of your soul."

A lot of things have shown me how people look at reality. Small talk, probably on the bus, books, movies, and social media especially! If I say I'm not intrigued by these takes, I'd be lying because some are too crazy to be brushed aside.

Now, I'm not here to be critical about the way people have chosen to think. Everyone has the right to believe whatever they want, and there's freedom of ideology, belief, faith, and many more abstract concepts. I agree with that.

But I know I'm not the only person who will freak out whenever I hear someone say that the body has no connection with something bigger than itself or that the physical body exists on its right?

It's probably not the way you're looking at it right now. I will not start arguing with anyone about their beliefs because

1

that will only be a severe waste of time and energy.

Even if we fail to admit it, there will always be the silent "Woah" moment in our lives. When we hear or see something out of our norm, we are in our minds like, "Woah?" And it then looks like the world replies, "Oh yeah, you haven't seen anything yet."

That is what will happen to me when I hear someone say that the physical body exists on its own. Because the concept is very sacred to me, I've had first-hand experiences that have made this concept too much of an apparent reality, only for someone else to tell me otherwise. Yeah, that's going to mess with my head for some time. Still, there's no time to dwell on the unimportant parts of life, like worrying about another person's values or opinions, especially when that person is a grown-up like you or even older.

The best anyone like me can do let you all know what it means to me and what knowing about it can do to change a lot of things about our lives.

Let's move on.

Finding out the Essence of the Spiritual Self

A lot of important things today are highly dependent on their essence. The question of essence revolves around so many things in this life. Money, fame, power, we often find ourselves asking, "what's the essence of all these?" And the same goes for what I'm about to discuss with you today.

What's the essence of the spiritual self? Why is it a thing or concept we may have to bother ourselves about? What is there to learn about it?

Finding out the essence of something may or may not change much about how a person would see such things. So even if a blockbuster movie was made, featuring all the movie stars in Hollywood about finding the essence of spirituality, a lot of people are going to enjoy the thrill and other cool stuff, but

3

who doesn't want to get the real message, still won't.

That, however, won't discourage me from letting you know the essence of your spirituality.
But wait a sec. I haven't even told you guys what spirituality means!

How forgetful of me!

So what is spirituality?

I like how Christina Puchalski, MD, Director of the George Washington Institute for Spirituality and Health, puts it. She says;

"Spirituality is the aspect of humanity that refers to the way individuals seek and express meaning and purpose and the way they experience their connectedness to the moment, to self, to others, to nature, and the significant or sacred."

And I couldn't agree less with her. I still don't understand what that means. Alright, I'll try to do some justice to it.

In humans or most humans (let me put it that way.) There's this feeling that there's that one thing beyond our sight and even beyond our understanding responsible for whatever happens to us daily. Deja vu? Coincidence? Some people feel it's a casual event, and it's gone out the window before they even know it.

But then, some people think that something beyond the natural is responsible for what has happened!

That's quite close to what I'm looking for, you see, that urge to find a connection between yourself and some forces that you feel may be in control of your life or specific events.

Another way I look at this is that we want to find out what that one connection is between the physical and spiritual, and we want to stay plugged in for as long as we can.

There are many ways people claim to access or connect to this innermost part of themselves that they seek to find.

Some may discover that their spiritual life is intricately linked to their association with a church, temple, mosque, or synagogue. In other words, religion.

Others may pray for or seek comfort in a personal relationship with God or a higher power. For some, their spirituality is tied to specific questions they ask themselves;

Am I a good person?

What is my connection to the world ?
What is the significance of my whole existence?
What is the best way to live my life?

Yet still and enjoyable is that others seek meaning through their connections to nature or art. Like your sense of purpose, your definition of spirituality may change throughout your life, adapting to your own experiences and relationships.

How do you think you're connected to your spirituality if you think you are?

Not one for me to answer, so I'll leave that to you. Having laid a fair foundation for what spirituality is, what is its essence? Why is it that important? Here are a few reasons why;

It defines the purpose of one's life; a lot of people are confused as to why they exist. Everyone has come to this world for a purpose, with something to achieve before they leave. No matter how "negligible" some people may see some things to be, that could be why a person was born to this earth, and getting in touch with your spiritual self, can prove very effective in helping you find your purpose in life.

Peace and Harmony: not only does spirituality promote peace and harmony between different people, but it also promotes an enabling environment for relaxation to reign within oneself. Or do you not know that battles are within the mind? Getting in touch with that spiritual self brings peace.

Promotes Love: I believe that we would not be able to love appropriately without getting in touch with our spirituality. We all know that love is beyond physical contact and romance. It entails a lot more; it is accepting and coping with the weaknesses of someone else or even yourself, having to forgive someone for a wrong they did to you. Having to make yourself uncomfortable to make another person comfortable without expecting anything in return is something one can do only when they are in touch with her spirituality. It takes more than physical attraction to do that. Trust me.

Courage: in life, people make a lot of mistakes. And some of those mistakes are meant to happen, no matter how grave. Ordinarily, we are scared of making these mistakes mainly because of the consequences we may have to face as a result of doing that. But the plain truth is this; spirituality teaches us not to be afraid of making mistakes because they're inevitable and necessary for growth. And I agree with that.

There are many reasons why humans should get in touch with our spiritual side. So much more than these just mentioned, but for space and time, I will have to conclude here and go on to other aspects of the subject of discussion.

RELIGION AND SPIRITUALITY

A lot of people tend to misunderstand religion and spirituality as meaning the same thing. I'm not saying they're entirely independent, but they're not the same.

More often than not, religion involves practicing rules, ethics, and certain beliefs in reverence to a supernatural being who may not be present but is believed to be in some unnatural way. Spirituality has to do more with yourself and your personal growth, which certain practices of religion can sometimes achieve.

Now that's where a connection comes in.

The practice of these specific laid down rules, ethics, and all that sort can help people know their spiritual selves. But that can only happen when such a person wants it and is determined enough to want to grow.

That's why we see so many people who are religious fanatics, but they're always up to no good. I hope you get what I mean; I'm not saying that people who try to get in touch with their spirituality are all good people, no one is perfect, but it's heartwarming to see those who try.

So it's good to be religious, no doubt. But there's no need to be religious when your spirit is lacking. To me, it's a total waste of time, so there's no need for it at all. But while you are religious, channel that religiosity to building up your spiritual life, and that's when you're going to enjoy it.

You know, sometimes or most times even, people are religious because they have no choice. They probably had their guardians or parents as an officer of the church or mosque and had to do the holy stuff, but their hearts weren't in sync with what they did.

Waste of youth.

EMOTIONAL HEALTH AND SPIRITUALITY

There's also a connection between mental health and spiritual health. You notice that many practices recommended for building up spirituality are similar to those recommended for improving emotional well-being because the two are connected, as do all aspects of well-being; emotional and spiritual well-being influence one another and overlap.

Once again, I'd like to reiterate that they're not the same. Spirituality is mostly about finding a meaningful connection with something much bigger than yourself, which can result in positive emotions, such as peace, awe, contentment, gratitude, forgiveness, and many other virtues. Meanwhile, emotional health is about cultivating a positive state of mind, which can broaden your outlook to recognize and incorporate a connection to something larger than yourself.

Thus, emotions and spirituality are different but linked, deeply integrated. Thus, emotions and spirituality are distinct but linked, deeply integrated.

IMPACTS OF SPIRITUALITY ON MENTAL HEALTH

The idea of spirituality as a whole has different meanings for different people, and spiritual beliefs are as many as the people who practice them. But, despite the difference in these beliefs, they all have something in common. They all affect our mental health.

Spirituality affects our mental health in so many ways. Spirituality mainly concerns your belief or a sense of purpose and meaning. It gives you a sense of value or worth in your life.

And like I've said before, contrary to what many people might think, spirituality and religion are not the same. But they indeed have a connection. You can be spiritual without belonging to a specific religion. Religious people abide by a particular faith and may be connected with specific groups or traditions, while spirituality is primarily a journey embarked on by only you.

So how does spirituality affect our mental health?
Spirituality has a significant influence on a high percentage of human decisions. It makes people probe into the nature of their being, the physical life, and the spiritual, which the bare eyes cannot behold.

Spirituality can help deal with stress by giving you a sense of peace, purpose, and forgiveness, so it often becomes more important in times of emotional stress or illness.

As much as spirituality can do good, it can also be detrimental to certain people, and we'll find out sooner.

To put it in a way that anyone can quickly grasp, here are some of the several ways that spirituality can be of support to our mental health:

You may feel a higher sense of purpose, peace, hope, and meaning.

You may experience better confidence, self-esteem, and self-control.
It can help you make sense of your experiences in life.
When unwell, it can help you feel inner strength and result in faster recovery.
Those in a spiritual community may have more support.
You may work at better relationships with yourself and others.

In addition, many people with a mental illness get a sense of faith and hope by talking with a religious or spiritual leader.

And the fact that some mental illnesses present themselves as times when people question their value or purpose in a way that leaves them feeling pessimistic and hopeless makes it extremely helpful to include spirituality in treating mental health difficulties.

Having said this, how can spirituality be detrimental to certain people, and what set of people are they in particular?

Even if we do not admit it, the truth remains that we live in a ruthless world with so many people up to no good out there. That is why some people may take advantage of emotionally vulnerable people while pretending to support their spirituality. If you're emotionally vulnerable, you can be more easily convinced to participate in harmful activities to improve your spirituality. Meanwhile, you're just being used or extorted. Concerning this, we must note that the spirituality here is not true; anyone should be able to spot what is fake and what is real. As for me, the yardstick is that true spirituality shouldn't cause me discomfort either spiritually or physically. I need to feel at ease to know I'm on the right track.

IMPROVING SPIRITUAL HEALTH

We need to talk about how we can improve our spiritual health. Having spoken about what it entails, its importance, and others, it all comes

down to how we can make this
spirituality work effectively for us.

And how can anyone make anything
work more effectively for them without
improvement? I honestly do not have an
answer to that.

Different approaches work differently
for other people. But the essential part is
that you do what gives you the most joy
and comfort.

These are some of the ideas one can use
to improve their spiritual health;

*Discover the things that make you feel
alive, joyful, loved, and in unison with
the rhythm of your soul.
Dedicate part of your day doing
community service.
Read inspirational books.
Try meditating.
Take a walk outdoors.
Pray – alone or with a group.
Practice yoga.
Play your favorite sport.
Dedicate quiet time to yourself.*

In concluding this section, I'd like to add
that a spiritual health evaluation is

sometimes necessary as a part of any mental health assessment. It is because mental issues like depression and substance abuse can be a sign or result of a spiritual void in your life. Therefore understanding the distinction between a spiritual crisis and a mental health issue is essential to getting to the root of the problem and finding the solution as well.

Do you see how the concept of spirituality cuts through every aspect of human life? I tell you for sure that growth is inevitable when you get in touch with that aspect of your life.

AFFIRMATIONS FOR SPIRITUALITY

1. I will not be critical of the way people have chosen to live their lives
2. I believe that there's more to life than the physical and social interactions
3. I cannot be 100% in control of my life
4. I've come to this world for a purpose

5. I have to find peace within myself.
6. I believe that it takes more than physical touch and romance to love
7. My mistakes are not who I am
8. I fear no mistakes.
9. I'm going to learn from my mistakes.
10. I believe religion and spirituality mean different things
11. I will not be oblivious to the connection between religion and spirituality
12. I am going to combine religion and spirituality to my advantage
13. I will not be a religious fanatic and be spiritually empty.
14. I have great value for my emotional health
15. I will channel my spirituality to making the right decisions and doing the right things
16. I will not take advantage of people who are emotionally vulnerable in the name of improving their spiritual life.
17. This cruel world will not allow me to be taken advantage of.
18. In practicing spirituality, I shouldn't have to feel discomfort.

19. I will embrace the connection I share with all life on this Earth.
20. I am always open to having a new experience of reality for myself
21. Little by little, I am connecting with my true purpose on Earth.
22. My age doesn't have anything to do with who I am or what I do; I am infinite.
23. I am connected with my soul every time of the day.
24. The universe hands me whatever I need at the right time.
25. I am a spiritual being have an earthly experience
26. I can tap into the abundance of the universe
27. I believe that whatever happens to me happens for my good.
28. The divine energy flows through me every day
29. I am worth whatever time I need to nourish my soul
30. I am open to loving my spirit more
31. I will always lend my ears to the voice of encouragement inside me
32. I am consciously and constantly aligned with my spiritual self
33. I am going to allow the universe to work through me

34. All of my thoughts, words, and actions are inspired by the divine
35. I am powerful enough to deal with negativity.

KEY POINTS

1. There's always more to life than what we see with our physical eyes.
2. Nobody has a similar experience of spirituality; people experience spirituality differently.
3. Every human being has a purpose in life. Some may or may not live long enough to achieve it.
4. Peace within should be your priority.
5. One has to be wary of how people describe spirituality to look.
6. Religion and spirituality do not mean the same thing but can be used together to improve the quality of our lives.
7. Improving our spiritual health is key to improving our mental health as well.

CHAPTER TWO

SELF AWARENESS

"It takes courage...to endure the sharp pains of self-discovery rather than choose to take the dull pain of unconsciousness that would last the rest of our lives."
-Marianne Williamson

Let me tell you a little story about myself.

It was my eighteenth birthday anniversary that day, and the day was almost over when my Dad called me into his room.

We were alone in the room, and he said to me,

"Son, I have a gift for you."

He then held my shoulders and spoke.

"This will be the greatest gift you have ever received. It is the key to your guaranteed success, and you have no choice but to use it well enough to yield the desired results, except you want to prove to me that bringing you up was a waste of time. Am I clear?"

I was perplexed. But I nodded slowly as my heart trembled in anticipation of whatever gift he had for me. I didn't want to be optimistic that the gift held the key to my success. Parents possess the art of exaggeration, so I had to keep the excitement low.

My Dad went into his drawer and slowly brought out something. I couldn't see it because he turned his back on me. And then the atmosphere began to feel like Hollywood as he began to shake the dust out of whatever he held.

He glanced at it and then turned to me, holding the object to his back. He walked toward me and said,

"You must use this every day and treat this with care if you seek good results."

It was a book, and the book's title was my name.
My Dad told me the book contained all I needed to know about myself and how I'm supposed to live my life according to it.

It seemed like a joke, but when I read the book and religiously followed the instructions on how I was supposed to love my life, that was when I realized that I could write books, and that's when I became the best writer in the world, winning five consecutive Pulitzer awards for writing and eventually becoming the wealthiest man on the globe after selling millions of copies of the books I've written.

What a story! Or most of you must be saying, what a lie!

But it seemed like an exciting and credible story, didn't it? Or at what point did you stop believing it?

Most definitely the point where I said I won 5 Pulitzer awards and became the wealthiest man globally. And you'll be like, oh yeah, this guy's making this all up.

Because yes! I concede that I'm making this all up because I've got something to point out to you.

Most people don't understand that they have to know themselves. Or let me put it this way: some people think they should know themselves because, why not? Am I not the one? Why shouldn't I know myself? Completely failing to realize that it is possible for them not to know themselves entirely and how they're wired!

Before we continue, I feel like there's a question that most readers would have in their minds. Maybe they don't have it per se, but it just takes a little jolting, and if I bring it to their attention, they're going to realize that they need to have an answer to it to understand what's going on here entirely.

According to the story I made up, I was 18, and my father still felt the need to give me a book about myself. Don't you think that's strange? I'm 18 years old; for heaven's sake, why would my father think that the best gift he'd give to me is a book about myself? At 18, what don't I already know about myself that I need a book to tell me?

Well, the truth is, I don't think we completely know ourselves enough to live life the way we ought to. And when that stage of self-realization comes in our lives, we must find out who we are and what we want.

Don't ask your Dad; that's just fiction. Even your friends would know you better than your Dad. It's your journey and yours alone. The path to self-determination is lonely, and that's how it's meant to be.

No one has the power to know you more than you, and if you don't know yourself, there might be a lot of complications

along the way if you don't act fast
enough.

WHY DO I NEED TO KNOW MYSELF?

I know, right? Why do we need to know
ourselves more than we already know
before? I mean, isn't it possible to live
with the information we already have
about ourselves and keep going on and
on?

Why does life have to get this
complicated?

Well, it's left for anyone to do as they
wish with their lives anyway. It's a
matter of choice, not anyone else's
choice, but mine and yours to live
however they want to.

But I still think it's fair to share my
opinion on why we should strive to
know ourselves. You know, to fulfill all

righteousness. The work has to be complete. I'm going to do just that.

Humans spend a lot of time worrying about our relationships with others and how they feel or think about us. But, the truth is the only relationship that matters in life is the one you have with yourself. Even if you're born twins, you will not die as one.

You're the only one going to be there for yourself when no one else can; it is only you, from the cradle to the grave. Not to sound selfish, but to emphasize why you need to know yourself.

These are some reasons why it is essential to know yourself.

Self-Love

If you know yourself, the good, the bad, and the ugly, that's a perfect starting point to accepting who you are - exactly as you are. It's going to feel like a challenge, trying to get aspects of your character that you're not a fan of, such as laziness and the sort.

However, if that is already a part of you and you've tried hard to change but cannot, it is important to honor that instead of denying it. It'll still be there, even if you decline it.

Applying a different approach could help too. Instead of trying to stop being lazy, learning to see the benefits of laziness, enjoying it, and not allowing it to work against you will enable you to embrace it as part of who you are and to, therefore, love it. You can move from love to nurturing, growing, developing, thriving, and flourishing.

Independence

When you know yourself, it makes you independent of how others feel about you. If you know what works for you, what is the best for you, and, therefore, what isn't - it becomes irrelevant what others might think and advise.

Like I said earlier, no one can know you more than you know yourself. You are the expert of your being. You are in charge of your thoughts and actions, and you are your personality.

Independence and self-awareness can also be linked to self-confidence. Thus, knowing who you are and what you stand for in life can help to give you a strong sense of self-confidence. Copy that?

Clear Decision Making

It is common knowledge that with knowledge comes insight and confidence, which are practical tools in decision-making (for both simple and complicated choices) to make it much more manageable. No one can doubt that when there's a level of understanding or insight about something, making decisions concerning such things becomes a piece of cake. So when we know ourselves to a great extent, making decisions that pertain to us wouldn't be much of a problem, and there's not going to be so much doubt about it.

There's this theory by Dr. Marriet Johnson that we all speak two languages: the language of the heart and that of the head. If they are aligned, it becomes effortless to make a decision. But if they're not, it just depends on your mood and what you think is right or wrong. And making decisions depending on your present mood can be very dangerous because attitudes can change in seconds. You don't want to make decisions based on fluctuating standards, do you? She further gives an example;

You are about to purchase a house and find one that meets all your requirements. However, something about the place makes you uneasy. You are unsure what it is, but it doesn't feel okay.

Having two contrasting dialogues in your head makes everything complicated. Today, your head tells you what to do, and you want to buy the house; tomorrow, it's your heart telling you not to go on with purchasing the home. Syncing your head and heart will give clarity, which supports easy decision-making.

These are a few of the many reasons why you need to know yourself. I don't know what else will convince you if you don't find any of these reasons convincing enough. I've done all I can for now.

So how do you know yourself?

How do you know anything at all? Pretty sure a vast percentage of us have gone through the process of trying to learn something, in one way or the other.
It could be in school, at the workplace, at home in front of the computer on YouTube, so many ways!

What are you trying to do there? You're trying to know something, and what are you doing to get that knowledge? You're learning! Simple!

That answers the question of how you know yourself. You know yourself through learning about yourself; the real question that should be full of content is how do you remember about yourself? That's where all the answers lie. Stick around, it's going to be an exciting ride, and you're surely going to go home with something you've never had before.

LEARNING ABOUT YOURSELF

Knowing your true self is one of the essential powers you can possess. When you know who you are, you always know what you need to do instead of seeking validation from others. It helps you to bypass the frustration caused by putting time into the wrong things.

Of course, life isn't a bed of roses and is supposed to be full of trial and error, but self-awareness lets you discover the best areas to experiment with.

Good knowledge of self will help you build confidence that cannot be shattered, and you will gain a deeper meaning of your purpose in life and eventually impact the world.

So, what is the secret to knowing oneself? Come with me as I explore tips to help you better understand yourself.

Be Still

You cannot and will not be able to discover yourself until you take the time to be still. Never underestimate the power of peace; many people don't have any idea of themselves because any silence scares them; all they want is the noise, the buzz; it's too sorrowful to be alone with all their flaws staring back at them. They always want the noise to overshadow their weaknesses.

But it isn't until you go to a quiet place and assess yourself while being completely honest with yourself that you will be able to see every aspect of your life clearly —the good, the bad, and the ugly.

Be quiet and discover who you are.

Distinguish Between Who You Are And Who You Want To Be

I understand that you already have a set idea of who you desperately want to be, but you might want to sit back and ask yourself, is this really who I am? Or are these expectations I've set for myself the ones I should meet? That picture you've already painted of yourself in your head might not be who you were designed to be. Knowing who you are will finally see where you and your specific gifts fit into the bigger picture. You can always be better than that person you desperately want to be.

And although there are many points along your journey to help you discover yourself, one of the best ways to start is to take a personality test. You can take it more than once, especially when it's been a while since you last took the previous one. And even if these self-evaluations aren't perfect, they do pinpoint your top areas of strengths or weaknesses, so you can focus on the change you were meant to bring into the world.

I tell you again; you can be so much better than that painting you already made in your head, so much better.

Find Out Your Strengths And Weaknesses

It might be the most challenging step in discovering who you are, but it's one you must take. No doubt, it takes a lot of trial and error to find out what you're good at, and you don't have to give up before you've made more than enough attempts, but you must realize that knowing when to quit is a gift that everyone needs to learn. You think leaving is not an option, no, no, no, not true.

You have to quit when you've put in so much time, and all your efforts fall shy.

Now, what is the measure for "so much time?" No one else but you can decide that, at least, you should know yourself up to that extent. But I want you to know that there's a big difference between quitting correctly and giving up. When you quit correctly, you're making room for something better. When I say something better, I mean something beneficial to you.

Take the hint when your actions begin to drain you rather than produce more passion and increase your drive to do more. That's a good sign it is time to focus elsewhere. Your strengths will show you who you indeed are, that's for sure. So build on them.

Follow Your Passion

The following passion of any kind is a good thing, and that's one of the aspects of your life that you need to pay attention to when it comes. The reason is that it shows an area of your life on which you need to focus more attention and resources.

If we're also talking about following your passion for work, that's a good one. And if it is having more passion for life, it's also a good thing.

Focus more on passion; I see passion as a gold mine because it makes you understand yourself better, allowing you to make a significant impact. Passion births effort and continuous effort produces results that produce a more profound discovery of your true self.

AFFIRMATIONS FOR SELF AWARENESS

1. I will embark on a journey to self-awareness and discovery.
2. No one knows me better than myself
3. I will focus less on what others think or say about me.
4. I will focus more on the relationship I have with myself
5. I will accept rather than deny who I truly am.
6. I will always try to see the silver lining in the dark clouds.
7. I love myself
8. I take control of my words and actions
9. I am my personality.
10. I am confident in who I am and all I stand for.
11. I will not base my decision-making on fluctuating standards.
12. I will always be ready to learn how to be self-aware.
13. I will not seek the validation of others.
14. I am bold enough to be still and face my flaws

15. I will not rely on the weaknesses of others to make me feel better
16. I will be completely honest to myself no matter the circumstances
17. I can be better than whoever I desperately want to be.
18. I will not give up easily, but I will know when to quit.
19. I will discover my strengths and build upon them.
20. I will follow my passion always
21. I will take advantage of any opportunity life offers me to make an impact
22. The journey to self-awareness is never-ending, and I am willing to go all for it.
23. I become aware of my innate talent every day
24. I continue to discover more of what makes me unique by the day
25. Being self-aware is one of my top priorities, and I work towards it every day
26. I always get to understand myself better every day
27. I will always allow myself to be myself no matter what it costs.
28. I am committed to finding out who I am and what I can achieve

29. I carefully monitor how I talk and think to myself every day
30. Whatever benefits me, I recognize and begin to nurture them
31. I know what I want in my life, and I work towards achieving them
32. I am striving to be fully aware of my feelings every day
33. If it's ever going to be, it's always up to me
34. It is one of my greatest desires to live each day fully aware of myself

KEY POINTS

1. No one can know yourself better than you do.
2. Learn to accept yourself the way you are sometimes.
3. Your improvement never ends.
4. Never rely on others' opinions about you.
5. Never make decisions based on your present mood.
6. You don't always need the noise.
7. You might not be cut out to be who you want to be. Accept that.

8. Forget about what you cannot do and build on your strengths
9. Your passion is your gold mine; follow it consistently.
10. The journey to self-awareness does not end.

CHAPTER THREE

SEXUALITY

"We have the means and knowledge to achieve universal sexual and reproductive health and rights. Meaningful progress is possible, it is affordable and it is vital."
~Ann M. Starrs, Co-chair Guttmacher-Lancet Commission.

In my book Spiritual Self-Care For Black Women, I talked a lot about sexuality and how it could be linked to spirituality. I know quite alright that the topic of sexuality can be vast, and that is why I'm writing about it again. In my previous book, I talked about many things; a brief history of human sexuality, a woman's sexuality, sexual development, puberty in girls, the concepts of honor killings, shame, and wrong teachings. Also, we could differentiate between sexual identity, sexual orientation, and sexual behavior, know the types of sexual orientation and gender identities, how sexuality affects spirituality: the link between the two concepts, and how to sync your spirituality with sex.

This time, you and I will be looking at sexual problems in women and living above the stigma of STDs. As we begin this emotional but enlightening ride, I encourage you to brace yourself. You're a strong black woman; always remember that.

Sexual Problems In Women

When talking about sex, I believe it encompasses both the pleasurable aspect and the, what should I call it, not-so-pleasurable aspect? It is no news that women's sexuality was once considered taboo to be spoken about. Still, women are changing the narrative worldwide now, and I believe this book and the rest of my books on sexuality will catalyze this cause.

Quickly, we shall be looking at the sexual problems in women but not without having an understanding of the sexual response cycle. Every human has a sexual cycle, both men and women, and all stages are passed through at different rates. In a situation where one step is missed, there is a problem. I'll briefly speak on the four:

Excitement Phase: This phase is also called desire, where a woman has this urge to engage in sexual activity like a charge in her body, prompting her to be responsive. It comes with quickened heartbeats and breathing and also flushed skin.

Plateau Phase or Arousal Phase: Immediately a woman enters the excitement phase, what could lead her to the next step largely depends on sexual stimulation. How she's touched or touches, what she hears and sees, the sort. In the arousal stage, the vagina secretes fluids in preparation for intercourse. It also expands while the clitoris enlarges and the nipples become erect.

Orgasm: This stage marks the peak of a woman's sexual response cycle, which has the muscles of the vagina contracting rhythmically and resulting in a mix of different emotions, with pleasure usually the first. It is also the climax stage.

Resolution: This is the last stage after a woman has successfully climaxed. It features her body relaxing, her clitoris, vagina, and nipples all relaxing and returning to their unaroused states.

As I have earlier stated, my dear black woman, any omission of these stages by your body will result in a sexual problem, and how do you know there's an omission? How d'you realize that there's a dysfunction in your sex life?

Symptoms such as spasms of vaginal muscles, absence of the excitement phase, experiencing pain during intercourse, etc., are a few of the numerous ways to know you have sexual dysfunction. If you experience any of these, my first advice to you is that you remain calm and brave as we continue. It should be easy for you to do; you are, after all, a black woman. In this book, types, causes, and solutions to female sexual problems will be discussed.

Female Sexual Problems

Dyspareunia: This is the abnormal pain you experience before, during, or after sexual intercourse.

Anorgasmia: This can be very frustrating for a woman who can feel excited but cannot experience orgasm and may have her desiring sex less. It is the term for delayed or infrequent orgasms. It's also the inability to have powerful orgasms or even just an orgasm.

Lack of sexual desire: A widespread problem in men and women. It stops the sexual response cycle before it even gets the chance to start, taking away any desire a man or woman would feel for their partner. At times, it can be temporary and ongoing at other times.

Sexual Problems can be very upsetting for men and women and can hinder sexual satisfaction, so it is trite that having known the types, we should understand the causes of these dysfunctions.

Causes Of Female Sexual Problems

Physical Causes: Gynecologic conditions such as vaginismus which causes vaginal muscle spasms, vaginitis, endometriosis, and other pelvic disorders, can make intercourse unpleasant.

Certain medications can also affect sexual functioning. Selective Serotonin-Reuptake Inhibitor (SSRI) group of antidepressants and chemotherapy may reduce your sex drive and affect your hormone levels. I used to know a woman whose name I cannot mention for privacy purposes. She was on antidepressants for quite a long time and, at the same time, was seeking solutions to a sexual dysfunction she had. The doctor diagnosed and found the antidepressants to be the cause. While this may affect some people, it may not affect others, so it's always best to seek professional help when you need to be on medications.

Hormonal imbalance may also be a cause of sexual dysfunction in women. My dear black woman, like it or not, your body is bound to go through several changes. Pregnancy, Menopause, and surgery are significant triggers of hormonal changes, and where there's an imbalance of hormones in your body, conditions such as vaginal dryness may surface, making sex painful to experience.

Other physical causes such as sexually transmitted diseases, fatigue, alcohol and drug intake, chronic diseases such as kidney diseases, heart diseases, radiation therapy, history of sexual and other types of abuse, and contrasting beliefs about sex may also hinder an extraordinary sexual experience.

Diagnosis Of Female Sexual Problems

To become fully in charge of your sexuality, you, my beautiful black woman, must be committed to seeing that things are right in your life, including your sexual health. Be vigilant and observant. When you notice anything unusual during sexual intercourse, I am here to plead and advise you to seek professional help.

When a sexual problem persists for weeks, it's only fitting that you stop ignoring or letting procrastination get the best of you and go for a checkup. Starting treatments on time can and has proven to go a long way in treating many illnesses. While some symptoms may persist for weeks, others may require immediate attention due to the advancement of the symptoms. Overall, it would help if you didn't hesitate to seek medical attention no matter how mild you may consider the signs to be. You're a brave woman, and I believe you can do this.

During diagnosis and tests, provide health care professionals with information regarding any underlying health condition you may have. In the absence of any, ensure to be as honest as you can with them. Also, please provide them with information about whether you're on medications or not and what medications you're on. Your gynecologist will perform a physical or pelvic examination and may refer you to other specialists for consultations.

Blood tests, imaging, and papsmear tests may also be carried out. You may be required to speak to a relationship counselor or mental health professional for psychological cases. You don't have to panic when seeking help, and always remember Lily Collins' words: "Asking for help is never a sign of weakness. It's

one of the bravest things you can do.
And it can save your life."

**Treatment Of Female Sexual
Problems**

I think the first step to treating sexual
problems is the acceptance of them.
Many people like to live in denial about
certain things in their lives to avoid
"depression," but the natural depression
comes when they find out it's too late. I
wouldn't like this to be your fate, my
beautiful black woman. You come first
in everything, and that includes your
sexual health.

When diagnosed with a dysfunction,
some problems require you to wait it
out, but if this isn't your case, you have
to swing into action immediately.

There are some physical solutions to try
out;

Arousal Techniques: Create time for
yourself and your partner, free of every

52

distraction. Increase stimulation and arousal by watching erotic videos or reading erotic books, masturbating, and using sensual massages.

Trying out different sexual techniques and discussing your sexual fantasies with your partner can help to boost sex and help you relax. A warm bath before sex is also good to try out, leaving you feeling relaxed.

Clitoral Therapy Device: This is an approved treatment device by the U.S Food and Drug Administration (FDA) for treating women with sexual dysfunction, particularly problems with arousal and orgasms. It increases lubrication when placed over the clitoris and enables a woman to orgasm.

Lubricants: If you experience vaginal dryness, vaginal lubricants should be the first thing you try. They do not need a prescription and can be found in stores. Scientists and I, likewise, recommend water-based products. Oil-based products are not the best choices as they might cause latex condoms to break. Trust me on this one.

Counseling: As discussed earlier, some sexual dysfunctions can be caused by trauma, stress, or other psychologically related causes. Using the services of a mental health therapist can go a long way in boosting your sex life. The therapist or counselor would help you identify negative attitudes and past traumatic experiences such as abuse and rape and teach you ways of overcoming these negative thoughts and experiences. The process can be painfully slow depending on how adverse the causes are, but believe me, if you're keen on overcoming these negative experiences, you will.

Surgery: Some sexual dysfunctions cannot be cured by physical solutions or psychotherapy, and in such cases, surgery is required. Specific issues like tumors and cysts require surgery for an improved sexual experience.

Prevention Of Female Sexual Problems

I've carefully listed a few methods to follow to prevent sexual problems from occurring within yourself as a woman or between you and your partner. Research has proven them helpful in curbing the spread of sexual problems in persons.

Communication: This is one of the secrets to a healthy relationship and healthy sex life. If you have underlying health conditions, be truthful to your partner and seek medical solutions. If the sex with your partner feels different, they should be the first person you talk to.

Meditations, Regular Exercises, Rest, and a Healthy Diet are principal to being relaxed and boosting your hormones.

Live a healthy lifestyle. Avoid smoking and alcohol. Also, attend regular and recommended checkups and health screenings.

LIVING ABOVE THE STIGMA OF STDS

Let's be brutally honest with ourselves; the names are pretty scary: Chlamydia, Gonorrhea, Syphilis, Human papillomavirus, Human Immunodeficiency Virus, Herpes, Genital warts, Crabs, and Trichomonas, to name a few.

Most are even almost impossible to spell, let alone be voiced. But the complicated phonics or spellings are the least of what people are concerned about when it comes to discussing sexually transmitted diseases (STDs), and no matter how long these STDs have been in existence, a lot of stigmas still hover around them.

Honesty Is Key

Just like some people hide their COVID-19 diagnosis from the public for fear of being judged and shamed, so do people diagnosed with STDs. If you ever feel alone because of an STD you're diagnosed with; I'm here to encourage you and let you know that no matter what you think, you should never have to lie about your condition. Understand that people will always talk and want to stigmatize you for having an STD, but they only penetrate you if you permit them. We'll get to a point where STDs no longer have to be associated with words such as "promiscuous" or "unclean," and you, my black woman, would be standing tall and proud by then.

Anyone can get an STI. It's even more common than people realize. If people catch infections just by handshakes, why should conditions from sex be more shameful?

Helping Yourself And Others

One mistake people make is believing that since STIs are very common, talking about them would be easy. In truth, it isn't. We've talked about why people shy away from the topic or admit being optimistic about it, but there's no way you'll help others if you see STDs as a form of a death sentence. People live their best lives with STDs and STIs, and so should you, my dear black woman.

I want you to raise your head high and promise to be everything but sad and in constant denial. You're owning up to everything you've passed through and arming yourself to help others.

A step to helping others is by being educated and knowing facts about STDs. That way, your fears would be allayed, and your confidence boosted. Joining support groups or creating one that talks about sexual problems and ways of overcoming them can also be helpful. It gives hope to people as well as yourself and is a safe space for meeting people going through similar circumstances and knowing their stories.

The next one I'm about to say might be absurd and straight to the point, but I'll say it either way. Date people with the same diagnosis as they would understand you better, and you would feel more at peace with them. Joining dating sites set up expressly to match people with STIs can speed things up and make you feel more at ease.

Talking about it on time also helps, including being honest with people, and your partner. If you recently started dating, you should be open and honest with them about your sexual health status before sexual intercourse, but only if you deem them to be worth it.

Importance of Breaking The Stigma

My dear black woman, I understand the stigma of STDs and STIs and how the fear of being tested positive might be so paralyzing, but I need you to realize that what is more dreadful is dying in silence.

If you feel something's wrong with your body, go for a checkup. If you think you feel okay, go for a checkup too. Either way, always go for checkups frequently. Some STIs are asymptomatic, while others may take years before manifesting physical symptoms, which would have been too late. Equip yourself with new information every day and live healthily.

Affirmations For A Positive Sexual Health

1. I am confident in my sexual life
2. I can do all I desire with my body
3. I will entertain only positive thoughts on my sexuality
4. Communicating with my partner about my sexual desires is straightforward.
5. I glow with sexual energy
6. Sharing my deepest sexual fantasies with my partner is natural.
7. I am worthy of the love I receive from my partner
8. I am safe and satisfied in my bed.

9. Sexual intercourse is fun for me.

10. Exploring my body makes me feel happy.

11. I have a healthy sex life.

12. My orgasms are frequent and powerful.

13. My partner can sexually arouse me and make me feel desired.

14. My genitals are entirely healthy.

15. I am willing to listen to my partner's sexual insecurities.

16. I am conscious of seeking ways to boost sexual experiences with my partner.

17. Rejection by a potential sexual partner will not make me feel lowly of myself.

18. My libido is alive!

19. I am a masterpiece, and so is my body.

20. I see sex as sacred and honor my partner.

21. I refuse to avoid my sexual desires but rather embrace them.

22. I feel no pain during sexual intercourse.

23. My partner makes me experience sexual pleasure and makes me feel loved.

24. I am in charge of my thoughts and feelings.

25. I am a natural at pleasing my partner and myself.

26. I know how to guide my partner to please me better.

27. My body is strong enough to fend off any sickness.

28. I am a sexy black woman.

29. My relationship with my partner is healthy and meaningful.

30. I am sexually satisfied.

31. I am constantly exploring and embracing my sexual desires

32. My sex life is a priority as it is necessary for my health and stress relief

33. I will be open to my partner about things that I enjoy and the things I do not

34. I only engage in passionate relationships while setting healthy boundaries

35. I am in complete control of my sexual thought, desires, and behaviors.

Key Points

1. The four sexual cycles women go through are the excitement phase, the arousal phase, orgasm, and resolution.
2. Symptoms of sexual dysfunction include unusual pain before, during, or after intercourse, spasms of the vaginal muscles, and inability to be sexually aroused.
3. Men and women should understand the causes of sexual dysfunction to know what to do.
4. Some physical causes of female sexual problems are gynecologic conditions, SSRI group antidepressants, STDs, chronic diseases, and hormonal imbalance.
5. Never ignore anything unusual going on in your body. If such a problem persists, seek professional help.
6. Being brave involves going for regular checkups.

7. Treatment of female sexual problems includes clitoral therapy devices, counseling, arousal techniques, lubricants, and in dire cases, surgery.
8. Some sexual dysfunctions can be prevented by living healthy lifestyles.
9. No one is immune to an STI. Be truthful about yours.
10. Joining or creating support groups, dating people with the same diagnosis, and talking about it helps you overcome the negative emotions of STDs.
11. Many STIs are asymptomatic, hence the need for regular health checkups.

CHAPTER FOUR

WORKPLACE

"There's no magic formula for great company culture. The key is just to treat your staff how you would like to be treated."
- Richard Branson, Founder of Virgin Group

If we're to be honest with ourselves, having to count the top 3 most important places in our lives, I don't think there'd be any way our places won't make it to the list for obvious reasons. If the place I go to make money to survive isn't essential, I wonder what other places will be. The White House? Some people could say so, but I'm not sure I'll be one of them.

Defining the workplace may seem absurd because the name already explains itself; nevertheless, I'd still like to determine what a workplace is.

In simple terms, a workplace is where a person performs jobs or tasks for an employer or himself, as the case may be. Workplaces vary from industries and can be inside a building or situated outdoors. They can also be mobile, and some people may have to work in different locations on various days. Still, technology has enabled people to work virtually without going to the office.

I will briefly explain the types of workplaces for the sake of knowing them and for the sake of distinction.

OFFICE

The office is a common, if not the most common type of workplace in the world right now, where employees of a company perform various tasks from a centralized location. Offices can take different forms and fashion. A company's office can be a whole complex, a single building, a compartment in a shared facility, or a section of a co-working unit. There are also what we call co-working sites. It's like a recourse for smaller businesses or companies who prefer to focus on their employees and customers first before their workplace. (Who knows, you might need that knowledge somewhere else.)

Home Office

Certain businesses do not need people to perform jobs or tasks in a centralized location and can benefit mainly from allowing their employees to work remotely. The necessary software, equipment, and training are available for employees who do their jobs wherever they might be. Some people could have a designated room in their home with a desk and computer to perform their work.

Flexible work schedules should be drafted and incorporated for a smooth-running business to ensure everyone works optimally. Provisions can also be made for staff who works remotely.

Distribution or Factory Center

People work in distribution centers in various industries, especially the food, apparel, electronics, and automobile industries. They are most likely to be located near the business's corporate office rather than separate locations, which is also possible in some cases.

Factory workers make the final product in the production line, while employees from the distribution center sort products sent to stores or customers.

Farm or Outdoor Location

As much as many industries require people to work in factories and distribution centers, some also need people to work outdoors! This set of people includes farmers, environmental scientists, park rangers, construction workers, law enforcement officers, and electricians; the list goes on.

I think these guys work the hardest because, unlike others who get to work indoors, protected from harsh weather conditions, these guys have to work no matter the weather condition.

Store

Various stores include supermarkets, boutiques, grocery stores, shopping malls, etc. The employees usually work indoors and often directly interact with customers. All stores are different, and factors warranting these differences include size, geographic needs, and location.

PURPOSE OF THE WORKPLACE

Workplaces serve different purposes depending on the type. But in general, they help businesses deliver their products or services to consumers efficiently. To further break these purposes down, corporate team members use their place of work as an avenue to collaborate and develop new ideas for manufacturing products and providing services for their customers. Businesses use factories to manufacture their products and distribution centers to organize the shipment of the product to retail stores or to the consumer. Stores exist for consumers to purchase products by giving a space for customers to see the product physically.

It's like a hierarchy of purposes for the workplace as they work hand in hand to achieve a specific aim.

Having spoken much about the workplace in literal terms, I want us to recognize that beyond those buildings and structures we just talked about, there's another definition. To me, the most important one. Which I call and we all know as the "Employee."

Oh! You probably thought I was going to talk about buildings forever. Oh no, I'm not. It will focus on what I think is far more critical than structures.

People!

It shouldn't come as a shock, or does it? We'd entirely agree that without the people, or should I say, the people who are capable enough, whatever structure exists would be outright useless. Don't we?

Or we could also say that these people would not be able to work effectively if these structures were not put in place, right? But systems do not fall from the sky, do they? I'm probably asking many questions now, but I can't help it because I'm trying to point out the truth!

The structures we may feel are so crucial for the human resource to work on are put in place by humans themselves! This is why the employee or employer if you put it that way (to me, they're all employees because even the employer is working for himself, which makes him an employee to himself), should always be at the forefront of concern. As we continue in this discussion, I'd like to expose you to a few things you can do to make the workplace a conducive one for you which would entail you knowing how to treat your fellow employees, recognizing your worth even when people want to intentionally be blind to it, taking note of the red flags, and also recognizing when to call it quits.

Hang in there!

WORKPLACE STRUGGLES

Not going to lie; this is an extensive issue. As vast as the whole of Asia if you ask me. As confined as the concept of the term "workplace" is, no one should be fooled to believe that everything that goes on there revolves around work only. The workplace is another world on its own. When you leave your home for work, it's like walking into another life where almost everything, the good, the bad, and the ugly, happens.

Real struggles go on in various workplaces. Efforts that not everyone knows about keep people up late at night, force people to take their own lives, and some struggles even go with some people to their graves!

There's a lot people have to endure for so many years that it even turns to some toxic sort of enjoyment because they don't want to lose their jobs, and it's unfortunate to say that as a black woman, some of these experiences may not be new to you. But we all hope to change the narrative, rewrite the story, and lend our voices, however loud they will be.

Everyone should know what goes on. Yeah, most people have an idea, but a lot of people still don't; they're probably too young and haven't gotten a job to know these things, but most of them will one day. They have to know what to expect and how to manage whatever comes their way, don't they?

Very well then, let's begin.

Sexual Harassment

Workplace sexual harassment is defined by The United States Equal Employment Opportunity Commission (EEOC) as "unwelcome sexual advances, requests for sexual favors, and other verbal or physical conduct of a sexual nature ... when this conduct explicitly or implicitly affects an individual's employment, unreasonably interferes with an individual's work performance, or creates an intimidating, hostile, or offensive work environment."
They then went further to say;

"The challenged conduct must be unwelcome in that the employee did not solicit or incite it, and that the employee considered the conduct as undesirable or offensive."

"Particularly when the alleged harasser may have some reason (e.g., prior consensual relationship) to think that the advances will be condoned, it is important for the victim to

communicate that the conduct is unwelcome."

Quite a lengthy definition involving specific ups and downs, but we all know the core of it, don't we? It shouldn't even be news to anyone above 18 to be modest. It happens everywhere!

Sexual harassment includes quite a wide range of actions, from verbal transgressions to sexual abuse or assault.

And although the victims are usually more women, we cannot rule out that men are sexually harassed too! In fact, throughout the United States, 21% of victims are men! That's, anyway, to make us understand that it can go both ways.

There's also what is called, Sexual Bribery, which is the demand of sex, any sexual activity, or other sex-related activity for a promise of a raise in work status or pay. This usually happens in an employment setting where a sexual relationship with a superior is made an explicit or implied condition for obtaining/retaining employment or its benefits.

Things like this happen out of their will but become the norm sooner or later.

Kiss up, Kick down

Have you heard of this situation before? You probably haven't heard the name but should be familiar with the experience. It is a term used to describe a situation where employees placed somewhere in the middle of the hierarchy of an organization are somewhat polite to those above them but means and abusive to those below them or even their colleagues on the same level!

Everyone ought to be treated equally, but these guys don't care. They exhibit what is also known as eye service to find favor in the sight of their bosses.

Gender Inequality

Don't tell me you weren't expecting to see this. I'm not even sure if I can label this work complete if this subject isn't discussed.

We already have a picture painted in our heads when we hear the term Gender Inequality, mainly about men and women not being treated equally due to certain factors like biology, psychology, or cultural norms prevalent in society.

But then, what about the workplace? I've said before that almost everything happens in the workplace. It's like a small society that mirrors the larger community it finds itself in and incorporates nearly everything good or bad into its system.

In 2008, female medical doctors who had just become qualified in New York State had a starting salary of $16,819 less than their male counterparts. That speaks volumes. Then come to think of what it entails for women who are black. Then we'd be merging the racial and gender factors, and that wouldn't be too nice a combination, would it? I'm afraid no. But it's the reality anyway. As in society, people are valued in the workplace by their gender, with the female gender usually being on the losing end. Despite whatever qualifications she may have or expertise she may exhibit.

Employers sometimes don't care about the potential they might miss out on to satisfy their conscience, which is wrong. If you ask me, whatever strategy a business owner may come up with, no matter how good that strategy is at ensuring growth and stability in the enterprise, if an all-embracing system isn't in play, that strategy may not achieve its full potential. People either fail to see this or see it and still ignore it.

The Toxic Workplace

I want to describe the toxic workplace as the result of the above factors and much more. It is like the term which encompasses all forms of ills in the workplace. Sometimes, not only employers or superiors who make up the toxic workplace. Employees play their roles as well in making the workplace unconducive for others. Sometimes these employees are even more trouble than their bosses and cause problems for them!

A "toxic workplace" refers to an office environment characterized by significant personal conflicts between coworkers whose actions can harm the overall productivity of whatever firm they work for. A toxic workplace is often seen as the result of poisonous employers and toxic employees who are motivated by their desire for personal gain (power, money, fame, or special status), using unethical means to manipulate and get on the nerves of those around them psychologically; the motives are to grow or increase power, money or special status or divert attention away from their awful performance and misdeeds at work.

These people exercise little or no care about the duty they owe the organization for which they work or their co-workers in terms of ethics or professional conduct toward others. They define relationships with co-workers not by organizational structure but by co-workers they favor and those they do not like or trust.

Working in a place alongside these kinds of people can toy with your feelings a lot. Even when you're not a direct victim of their toxicity, just seeing them display their toxic traits daily at work can sometimes be tiring or even traumatic.

Just imagine watching a dedicated co-worker who probably works harder than everyone else in the office being mistreated, underpaid, slandered, and the likes because of her skin color or because she didn't say yes to the sexual demands of her boss. That can do a lot of psychologically damaging things to anyone who has a conscience. Then what if, just what if you were a direct victim of such toxicity in the workplace?

It would help if you were on the lookout for sure signs in trying to identify toxic workplaces. If you're not already aware of them, I'm here to help, always! You should know that you can count on me anytime, any day! Here are a few signs that you notice in a toxic workplace;

Fatigue and Ill Health

Toxic workplaces will often make you feel stressed out, tired, and ill due to the level of stress you may be trying to endure. So, if you find yourself calling in sick often or constantly feeling drained and exhausted, it may indicate that your work environment is negatively affecting your health.

Lack of Enthusiasm

While at work, scan your office or work area well and search for signs of genuine happiness. It can equal toxicity if you're unable to notice positive conversations or employees socializing. This lack of motivation can rub off on everyone in the workspace, creating a more significant problem.

Low Turnover Rate

If you begin to observe a low turnover rate at your company or your workspace, it may point out that other workers have picked up on the toxic vibe in the workplace. Poor morale, sickness, and an overall lack of enthusiasm will certainly lead employees to seek employment opportunities elsewhere.

Stifled Growth

If your organization doesn't offer learning opportunities or mentorship, I'm afraid they may not be invested in your growth. Of course, it may not be the company's responsibility to motivate you to continue learning and improve yourself, but the lack of support can indicate a toxic workplace. They're only interested in taking from you but not adding to you. That's toxic enough.

COPING WITH WORKPLACE TOXICITY

While we have learned a few signs to note if your workplace is toxic, it's also essential to know how to handle these struggles if you do not plan to quit anytime soon. To me, leaving is always an option. It only depends on how long a person is willing to endure or when such a person finds an alternative.
We should also have in mind the fact that what works for others may not work for you. So do well to figure out what works for you, and don't kill yourself trying to fit in a particular style.

Having said quite enough, here are a few ways to deal with a toxic work environment.

Find Support

Support comes in handy in any situation, toxic workplace; it's essential to have people who stay by you no matter what position you find yourself in. You should see this support outside your place of work rather than in your workplace. Because while you may feel uncomfortable venting to your colleagues at work, your support system outside work allows you an outlet to express your emotions and frustrations without reservations.

Stay Positive

Spending so much time around toxic people can negatively affect your mood. Staying positive should be your priority, even if you don't find yourself around uplifting personalities, to keep you from never-ending negativity. Always remind yourself of the good part about your job and look for the good in as much as you can. When you're always focused on what you're grateful for, you're not going to allow the negativity to get to you.

Also, remember that seeing the good in something is not equal to being utterly blind to what you're not comfortable with.

Take a Break

There should always be time to step away from your duties. Taking a short break gives your brain time to rest. Take walks, meditate or eat a healthy snack. Just try as much as possible to leave your workspace for a short period as it can improve your mood and overall productivity when you return to work.

Meditate

Take a few minutes out of your work break to meditate as it helps to cultivate peace and calm in your mind. Take deep breaths in a rhythmic pattern, focusing on every breath you take and relieving any tension and stress.

Surround Yourself With Positivity

There are different kinds of personalities you find in the workplace. It's for your good that you hang around the positive ones. Having them around can help you survive toxicity. Make it a goal to spend as much time as possible with them. You are providing support for them and socializing with them throughout the day.

Quit

If you can't take it anymore, it's OK to admit that you can't. Don't force things. But before you leave, make sure you have some other opportunities and that you're a hundred percent sure of the decision.

AFFIRMATIONS

1. I am a masterpiece, and I am good at what I do.
2. Amidst toxicity, my self-worth remains intact.
3. I will not be a reflection of a toxic workplace
4. I am in control of my actions and responsible for the consequences
5. I have no room for negativity
6. I will not be a contributing factor to a toxic work environment
7. I am a smart and intelligent black woman
8. There's always an option for me; I will always have a choice
9. I refuse to be objectified by anyone, whoever they might be
10. I will always see the good in everything
11. I am not a moron; I will not be blind to my struggles
12. I am not a party to gossip and small talk.
13. I am the boss of my life
14. I am a pillar of support to others.
15. I am surrounded by positivity
16. I am not stagnant; I crave growth.
17. There's always a reason to be grateful

18. I have a bright future
19. I radiate good energy amid the toxicity
20. I will always be productive and wise with my time because there's a lot to achieve
21. I strive to be consistent at work
22. I choose to remain positive because success begins with the mindset
23. I am letting go of what I can't control to focus on the things I can
24. I will not always feel my best every day, and that's fine.
25. I will make mistakes along the way, and that's fine and normal
26. I will not make rest a luxury but a priority for me
27. Where I work and what I work as don't define my worth
28. I will always make time for family and friends no matter the schedule
29. Even when it gets hard to do, I treat every co-worker with respect
30. I will not allow anyone to take me off course on any day at work
31. I will remain calm when dealing with difficult people

32. When I need to be, I will be honest with my colleagues and will not be offended when they are with me.
33. I will always be confident when sharing my ideas and talent
34. I can go after whatever I want; I have given myself that permission.
35. I embody excellence.

KEY POINTS

1. Society and all its components reflect in every workplace
2. There should always be a limit to endurance
3. Psychological stress always has a way of affecting you physically
4. Find support and surround yourself with positivity always
5. Adopt practices to cope with toxicity while searching for a better place
6. Always know when to quit.

CHAPTER FIVE

FRIENDSHIPS

"Remember that the most valuable antiques are dear old friends".
-H. Jackson Brown, Jr.

We had to get to this point, ladies; it is essential to get to this discussion because if we're talking about life, we've got to talk about friendship. If we're going to be talking about how to improve lives, one of the focal points for discussion has to be FRIENDSHIPS.

In my own opinion, I think this aspect of human life is not given the needed attention. What's more? The word is even misused; it is misunderstood most of the time! It has been treated so casually that people no longer know the true meaning of friendship. And that is why they use it to describe almost every relationship.

But the truth remains that there are words for specific situations. You don't have to call it friendship, your colleague at the desk opposite you, doesn't have to be your friend, the guy or the girl you share a desk with at school doesn't have to be your friend, even your roommate doesn't have to be called a friend! What other scenarios are there? Just name it. Many people misunderstand the concept of friendship and become surprised when people expect to turn up for them in certain situations because they called friends to fail to do so. No girl! She's not a bad friend, she was just never a friend, and that's not her fault!

Why not define relationships properly and stop taking things as you feel or think they are instead of taking things as they are?

There's so much to discuss on the subject, and we'll approach it to step by step. Let us know what friendship is, stop forcing relationships, and improve our lives!

WHAT ARE FRIENDSHIPS?

Friendships can be defined as relationships of affection that exist mutually between people, a more vital form of interpersonal relationship than an "acquaintance" or an "association," such as a classmate, coworker, neighbor, or colleague. Like I said earlier, we should not be too quick to qualify these other relationships as friendships because, most of the time, they do not turn out to be so.

A person may realize he has developed a strong bond with another person over the years without even knowing it. That's where the term "best friend" comes in. Many people in today's world want to choose that kind of friendship. But to me, that kind of friendship chooses you both! It is not a conscious effort; it just happens consistently and will take a while before any of the parties eventually realizes that Oh! This guy's been my buddy for so many years; how did I not know? Yeah, you didn't know

because that's how it's supposed to be;
you don't force it.

Different people have established
various definitions of friendship, and I
will talk about them. But it amazes me to
see so many rules, theories, and the sort,
bordering around something that I feel
should be natural!

For instance, many people say "three is a
crowd," and therefore, three people
cannot be best friends or close friends.
They even go as far as drawing
conclusions on trios and telling them it'll
never work because the world says
"three is a crowd." They have specific
reasons to back their claims, which may
be valid, but I still have many questions!

Friendship results from human
emotions, what people feel for each
other, which hardly anyone but
themselves could decipher. So I wonder
how people can make these
condescending theories about friendship

and want to quickly draw lines or plant red flags on a certain kind of friendship.

Most of the time, a trio may not turn out well and doesn't make a trio a friendly one to run away from when it comes naturally. There are friend groups of 5 to 7 that flourish for years and would probably be the same for long, so what's all these fusses about friendship and the metrics brought about by different scholars or whatever they might be?
In my opinion, it all comes down to you, girl. How do you feel about the friendship? That's all that matters and nothing else! You have to put yourself and your feelings over that of the psychologists who are entitled to their opinion too, but those opinions don't have to be a standard for your friendship. If you're in a trio and it makes you feel good, loved, and cared for, choose that over what anyone has to say because it is a personal issue, and the opinion of others doesn't matter much.

FORMS OF FRIENDSHIPS

This is an aspect of this subject that so many people have had so many different takes on. I'll tell you the simple fact; inconsistency is annoying because when a concept has too many opinions about it, it may lose its authenticity, and the real meaning will be lost along with it. Why not? So many people have a lot to say, and a good percentage of them may be wrong and misleading, unfortunately.

Be careful not to miss the point and make the best of whatever works for you because that matters the most.

For this part, I'd like to toe the path of the great Greek philosopher Aristotle. He says that there are only three kinds of friendship. And I love the distinction. It reflects what happens in our reality today—an absolute truth.

So What Does He Say?

According to the Macedonian-born Greek philosopher, the three kinds of friendships that exists are:

- Friendships of Utility
- Friendships of Pleasure
- Friendships of the Good

These three kinds of friendships will be explored below for a better understanding.

Friendships Of Utility

These kinds of friendships exist between two people who have found out that they will consistently be of benefit to each other. It exists between you and someone who will be helpful to you somehow and vice-versa. Without those benefits, the purpose of such friendship will be defeated.

For example, you've got a co-worker, preferably working at the next desk, which helps you work on stuff when they're too much for you to handle. You help cover for him when he's out somewhere else for a different engagement, you know, stuff like that, and it goes both ways, consistently, not one doing more than the other. That is what Aristotle regards as a friendship of utility.

More like an *"I scratch your back, you scratch mine"* kind of relationship between two people.

I once had a friend during the COVID-19 pandemic, where we all had to work remotely. He was always there to call me for impromptu meetings we had when I happened to be offline, and I would also do the same. On the day he couldn't be online to attend meetings, I would cover up for him; on the days I couldn't be online to participate in discussions, he would do the same.

We had small talks about the duty we had placed on ourselves, but we were both aware of what we suddenly became close to and had unconsciously set limits that we didn't venture beyond. With the pandemic being over, we didn't have much need for each other anymore, and though we tried to start something when we both saw each other's life, the spark wasn't present anymore. The use we both had for each other was no longer present, so sooner or later, we had become like strangers again.

It shouldn't be surprising how we both "fell off" if you want to go out that way. A need brought us together. We both had something to benefit from each other, and that's why we became close in the first place. And with that thing not being in existence anymore, there was no need for friendship anymore, so even if we tried to breed something after the market was gone, it might not have worked because there was no need for the company anymore. We understood that and accepted it the way it was. One critical thing I want you to note about this story is that we understood what we both had back then during the pandemic and realized that we couldn't have that chemistry anymore since there was no spark to it. So we both did not complain that we were slowly drifting apart because we both knew what we became friends for, and it had ended. So what's the need for any charade? We both continued living like nothing ever happened between us during the pandemic.

It's that simple how this kind of friendship works when there's understanding. Any company would work when there is a mutual understanding between both parties about precisely what friendship both have.

Now, I am dropping a hint on how big of a role understanding plays in friendship. Let's move on.

Friendship of Pleasure

Well, as the title connotes, this friendship exists between two people who tend to enjoy the company of each other. The most common scenario is when you want such a person because they are a funny person or are willing to do something to make you feel good. Maybe they have a video game you can play during your free time and be on the same football team or whatever sport you both enjoy.

It's a mutual relationship, so you would also have something to offer to such a person to make that person want to be in your company.

A question, however, could arise as to where the "Friends with Benefit" card would come into play. Whether in the first category or this one. The reason is that, with regards to the first type, you could use each other for sexual satisfaction, and with the second type, you could like each other because of how you make yourselves feel in bed.

I feel the connection between the second kind of friendship would be more robust. This is because, according to the great Aristotle, for the company of pleasure, we would like more than one aspect of the friends we tend to keep for fun. Apart from the sexual satisfaction, one party provides, one might also like his wit, her compassion, or his flirty manner, for instance. On the other hand, friendships of utility exist mainly because the person can help us somehow. And without both parties providing almost the same assistance, that friendship would not work as it is meant to.

Friendships Of The Good

These kinds of friendships have their foundation in mutual respect and admiration. These friendships take much longer to build than the other two types discussed above, and as a result, they're also more powerful and enduring.

These kinds of friendships often materialize when both parties recognize that they have similar values, goals, and ambitions, have similar visions for how the world (or at least their lives) should be, and both work towards achieving what they plan on achieving, Not infrequently. More often than not, this kind of friendship begins in childhood, adolescence, or college, even if plenty still forms after that, too.
These kinds of friendships are primarily unconditional.

They're not there because you have a use for them; you're not here because they take pleasure in being around you; they're there just because you're you and because they mean a lot to you. Such a friend doesn't have to do a thousand and one thing for the other party to kindle the friendship, nor have to do whatever the other party enjoys gaining this friendship. This friendship is purely genuine, and there are no strings attached.

This friendship encompasses all other companies and should be the standard for a true friendship.
This is what I regard as friendship in the first place. Because I value friendship so much, any other relationship named "friendship" doesn't portray what friendship truly is, is not and will never be friends to me.

According to Aristotle, whom I agree with, the third kind of friendship is the most important among the three types of friendships. These are friendships founded on mutual respect for one another, appreciation for each other's qualities, and a solid will to assist others in need because they believe in each other and recognize their greatness. To me, this is the only relationship that should be termed friendship.

The first two types of friendship can be broken or lost easily. The driving force behind those kinds of relationships is one's utility and pleasure. These friendships will probably fade off when benefits are achieved or a change of common interest. However, companies based on goodness are usually long-lasting.

And people that'll value your friendship, not because of what you have to offer or what they stand to gain from you, but for genuine reasons, are hard to find and develop, and If you happen to have more than a handful of friends based on goodness, you are indeed blessed. My mother always says, *"Friends will tell you what you desire to hear, buts good friends tell you what you need to hear."*

Having looked at the three kinds of friendships Aristotle spoke about, how about we talk about the company's qualities?

The subject is broad, and if anyone plans to cover everything up on friendship, such a person would have to write a full-fledged book.

So let's move on to our next subject for discussion.

QUALITIES OF A FRIEND

It is vital to note that when it comes to friendship, you must never choose quantity over quality. That's like a taboo. Having ten people you call your friends, or you think you are your friends when they're not, is much worse than having three genuine people who know the value and worth of friendship.

The following are some of the qualities you would want to look out for when breeding friendships with other people;

Loyalty

Do you have a friend who forsakes everything to help you at the point of your need? That is someone whom you can call a friend and not a person you should play with. Hold them tight and close because their type is rare. Always being there when we need them the most, helping to lighten our burden, providing a shoulder to lean on, and also helping to shoulder the inevitable hurdles, stresses, and crises that life throws at us. They can transform what seems to be an unfathomable mountain into a small hill that can be easily accessed. They are always there to make things easy.

You shouldn't trade such a person for anything in the world because it won't be easy getting such a person ever again.

Trust Worthiness

No friendship should leave trust out of the list. That box must be ticked! Every relationship needs trust as its bedrock and foundation to stand firm. Friendship is not an exception when every relationship is mentioned. Therefore, one of the qualities of a good friend is that they are trustworthy and genuine.

Do not be ashamed to tell someone you call a friend about your weaknesses, imperfections, or shortcomings. You should trust them enough to keep it a secret when you tell them to, and if you don't, you should reconsider your friendship with such a person.

Acceptance

A friend will accept you for all your perfections and imperfections. And you're not going to feel uneasy being in their company because they have made you feel safe and comfortable, irrespective of your shortcomings.

Even though you are not in any way perfect hence, you can be yourself around them. That's one of the pleasures a good friendship allows you to enjoy. You can afford to be yourself around them because they have acknowledged and accepted that not everyone can be perfect, and you happen to be among them. A good friend will get you despite your flaws and love you wholly.

Listening Ears

No one doesn't need someone to listen to them actively. Imagine being in a situation where you need your friend to listen and pay attention to what you have to say, but they do the exact opposite. It would, in many ways, make you sad, wouldn't it?

And then a friend who always lends a listening ear to what you have to say engages with you and even offers a solution to any problem you may have been experiencing. Isn't that blissful? It sure is!

Reciprocity

There are a lot of qualities to be considered when building friendship, but I may have to draw the curtains here. And there's no better quality to conclude with than this.

We must understand that in everything we do with other people, striking a balance in any relationship is essential, especially the one of giving and taking. The quality of a good friendship is that reciprocity exists, no one should be selfish about most of their needs, and this will lead to a relationship where both parties will be satisfied.

This does not mean that one friend carries all the burden in the relationship; it means that, while one has the ball, the other does too. When the support comes from just one side of the relationship, the supporter will give up at some point.

Some friends would outdo the other, but this is fine so long as the other party reciprocates the gesture because some people are naturally born to give more. To me, the purpose of friendship will be defeated without reciprocity.

Why do I have to lend anyone a listening ear when they won't do the same for me?

*What's the need to accept a person
when they will not accept you?
Why would anyone want to be loyal to
someone else if that person will not
return the energy?*

These are not selfish questions but
reasonable questions that need to be
adequately answered before one
ventures into any friendship that will
most likely not bring satisfaction.

It's that simple. If you can't return the
energy, then there's no need to give you
in the first place.

To conclude, all these qualities you wish
to see in other people, you should see
first in yourself. Aside from finding and
being with a good friend, you have to be
a good friend so that compatibility can
exist. If you're not willing to be a good
friend to a person, then there's no need
to make friends with such a person, and
that's on, period!

AFFIRMATIONS

1. I am a great friend
2. I can tell my friend anything I want to
3. I attract amazing friends to my life
4. I am not ashamed of being myself around my friends
5. My friends are one of the sources of happiness in my life
6. let go of toxic relationships with ease
7. I reciprocate in the best way I can
8. I can rely on my friends always
9. I have deep connections with my friends.
10. New people come into my life at the right time
11. I will always offer support to my friends
12. I will always lend a listening ear to anything they have to say.
13. When I can, I'll always be there for my friends.
14. I will attract the perfect friends when I'm ready to make new friends.
15. Every day, I attract positive and amazing people.

16. I will not run after people who will let me down.
17. I'm imperfect; my friends are, too; it doesn't get to me.
18. I always feel safe around my friends as they feel around me.
19. I make friends that I genuinely admire
20. All my friends and beautiful in their unique way
21. I will always make sure to set healthy boundaries
22. I constantly let my friends know how much they mean to me
23. I will always be able to talk to my friends about something
24. I can say no to my friends, and they'll understand
25. My friends do not judge me, and I also do not consider them
26. I can always make new friends when I lose the old ones
27. I genuinely want the best for my friends, and they want the same as well
28. I attract friendships that bring me joy
29. No matter how long a company lasts, it'll always add value to my life

30. I can walk away from friendships that cause me pain
31. I will always value positive relationships.
32. I attract healthy and worthy friendships.
33. I forgive myself for all the times I stayed in toxic friendships.
34. I do not attract friendships that trouble my soul.
35. I attract friendships that align with my goals in life.
36. I am not afraid to move away from friendships that make me less of myself.

KEY POINTS

1. Friendships happen naturally.
2. Everyone has to play their part in a friendship
3. One must be willing to sacrifice in friendships
4. Friends ought to learn how to accept each other's weaknesses
5. A friend in need is a friend indeed.

CHAPTER SIX

FINANCES

"I believe that through knowledge and discipline, financial peace is possible for all of us."
-Dave Ramsey

We all think of one thing when we hear "Finance." Do I need to tell you? Money, of course!

Money? Who on earth doesn't take money seriously? I'm yet to find anyone who doesn't, honestly. That's to show you how much importance money holds in the world today.

But to tell you the truth, the word finances holds much more than money. Of course, money is part of it, but there's a lot to finance beyond just having money at your disposal. And we're going to be looking at what's more.

Finance studies the discipline of money, currency, and capital assets. It is related to but isn't the same as economics, which is the study of production, distribution, and consumption of money, assets, goods, and services. I don't want to sound too educational, so it has to be broken down into bits where we can deal with our concerns about finances because it is a vast topic.

There are mainly three areas of finance generally.

We have Personal Finances, defined as "the mindful planning of monetary spending and saving, while also having in mind the possibility of future risk." Personal finance usually involves:

- Paying for education.
- Financing durable goods such as real estate and cars.
- Buying insurance.
- Investing.
- Saving for retirement.

The major areas of personal finance are income, spending, saving, investing, and protection.

Then we have Corporate Finances, which deals with the actions that managers take to increase the firm's worth to the shareholders, the sources of funding and the capital structure of corporations, and the tools and analysis involved in the allocation of financial resources. So this is finances catering for a business or a corporation.

And then lastly, we have the public finances, which describes finance as related to sovereign states, sub-national entities, and associated public entities or agencies, which means finances relating to nations or states.

With all that has been said so far, it should be pretty clear what aspect of finances we're about to discuss. Not that the others don't affect our daily lives in specific ways, they do. But we will deal with aspects closer to our personal lives and finances.

With money being a necessity in today's world, it has become essential to know how to spend when we earn.

And this is not restricted to a particular class of people. Everybody needs to learn the art of money, whether you make a million dollars a month or just a thousand. Everyone needs to know the workings of money and how to manage it. Because failing to do so, will undoubtedly bring about waste and other unforeseen costs that may accrue to money mismanagement.

So, here we go! The big topic!

PERSONAL FINANCES

Concerning personal finance, the term is mainly used to describe the financial management of a person or a family's resources. It is made up of how one manages their money through expenses, investments, and savings, taking into consideration various unforeseen life events and risks.

Other personal finance aspects include banking, budgeting, retirement, insurance, estate planning, and more.

The term stands for the entire financial industry in a person's life, which encompasses all the bodies that offer financial services to an individual.

The main focus of personal finances is on meeting the financial goals of an individual or a person, both long and short term. Whether you have enough money for your monthly bills or want to plan for your retirement, it all depends on how well you can sort out your finances.

Suppose one has attained a certain level of financial literacy. In that case, it plays a massive role in helping such a person to know the difference between financial decisions that will be beneficial and that which will be detrimental to their financial future.

Having a plan for your finances will help you meet your short- and long-term needs without exceeding your income limits.

The truth is, it's better to start planning your finances sooner than later. So, you shouldn't be left out in this race, my beautiful young black lady. You have to take steps to improve the quality of your life, and this is one of them. So I urge you to follow through, as there are many things to be learned here.

The Essence of Personal Finances

There are specific reasons why knowing about our finances is important. A few out of many will be treated below;

Meeting Money Needs

Everyone has to understand this simple truth. Money issues are beyond what most of us know. We must look at the bigger picture when we approach this subject. This way, we can think beyond just going to work and making money at the end of the month or however we get paid.

You should be able to ask yourself,

"What comes after making that money? Do we spend?" Well, this shouldn't be the case.

When we ask ourselves these questions, our answers are supposed to help us draw out plans that establish how much our income is, what our expenses are, what plans we may have, as well as our future financial objectives. That is how you think beyond just working to earn money because that's not all there is to life.

Managing Your Income

If one fails to plan for their income, they will either overspend or spend on unnecessary items. Still, with a proper financial plan, one can manage theirs effectively.

Planning will enable you to spend your money on what is necessary and save or invest the rest.

Furthermore, managing your income will help you draw out a priority list, giving you an idea of the expenses to take care of. You can also effectively know how much is necessary for tax payments, savings, or clearing your monthly bills. Ain't that cool?

Budgeting, Spending, Saving, and Investing

Financial stability doesn't wholly depend on having a fat paycheck at the end of the month. That is one butter truth most people don't want to accept. A person who earns a $500,000 salary every month can still be living in a substantial financial crisis if they fail to plan for that income. It is because they may be spending much more than they are earning, sometimes without knowing about it.

On the contrary, a person earning less than 500k a month could still live a more financially stable life than the former. It will be so if such a person has drawn out a suitable plan for his income, saves, and lives within his means. It's that simple.

Good personal finance skills help you to understand how much you earn, what your monthly expenses are, and how you can budget within that income.

Many people may regard it as living stingy. Still, I call it sticking to what your budget indicates, and it does a great deal in helping one avoid so many overspending temptations that they otherwise would have ignored.
For example, you will be able to resist the temptation of purchasing a luxury gadget to fit in a friends club by looking at your budget and checking if that can fit into your list.

If your income doesn't allow it, or you have some other things planned, you can forgo the shifting. You can achieve this if you have a budget and stick to it diligently. If you don't have a budget drawn, I'm afraid you will have nothing to stick to and end up overspending and having a lot of regrets later on.

As Dave Ramsey said, *"Don't spend more than you earn!" This is a simple rule you must adhere to live a financially comfortable life."*

Having the Family Financially Secured

Somewhere near the top of every woman's priority list is financial security for them and their families. Everyone wants to be assured that they can cater to the money needs of their family, in a failing economy or not.

It even hurts to think of their families suffering due to a lack of money, especially when they are not around to help. It is the most common reason people struggle to earn enough money that can offer them a sense of security for years to come.

Many people fail to realize that the answer does not lie entirely in how much one earns but also in how much income is planned. The truth is, if you want to have financial freedom and security, you must learn to make sound financial plans.

Lastly, with healthy insurance policies and investments, you and your family won't suffer financially.

Keeping Off Bad Debts

Having little debts is not much of a problem. But being overly in debt is where the problem lies and can be very dangerous to your future finances. It's necessary to be able to manage one's obligations in such a way that guarantees that no damage is done to your future financial stability.

Wanting to grow your wealth quickly is equivalent to knowing how to manage your debts, which is why personal finance is critical to ensure this happens.

One way to stay off debt is to avoid overspending or spending more than you earn.

Improving the Standard of Living

One vital importance of financial planning is helping you improve your living standards. But how can personal finance help you achieve this feat?

The truth is that the more you plan for your finances, the more your savings will be. This means that instead of more money going to unplanned expenses, more will be saved. Higher savings will enable you to manage during financially challenging times.

To conclude, I must say.

Studying your finances is one big step to having a stable financial future. Very few are aware of this.

And although some will not realize early enough to make a change until they are too deep in a financial crisis, I can only hope that my beautiful black ladies wouldn't disappoint me and be one of those who will always ask, "why is personal finance important?" after this discussion, change for the better now, and impact your future finances before it's too late.

RULES OF PERSONAL FINANCE

Having spoken about the need for personal finance for our young black women who will change the world, some rules ought to be followed to the teeth if possible to ensure that our finances wouldn't be in chaos at the end of the day.

Let's peruse the rules together, and you'll promise me you'll practice them. I believe you can! Because a black woman can do anything, she is determined to do to make her life better, and I can't help but be elated being able to play my part in all these. Yay! I'm pumped! Let's go!

Have a Goal

If you have no defined goals, it won't be easy to know what personal financial success entails. Define your destination, and then create a realistic step-by-step plan that helps you achieve them.

Start Saving Early

Time has a way of being against us and can also be our best friend. When saving, time is going to be your best friend when you start saving early enough, say in your early 20s. And not only will you have more time to build wealth (even on a modest salary), but you'll also have more time for compounding interest to work its magic.

Distinguish Wants From Needs

People find it hard to separate their wants from their needs. It may sound absurd, but these are issues, and it only leaves them in a constant state of financial unrest. But I want you to understand that human needs are pretty simple — food, clothing, shelter, health care, reliable transportation, etc. To me, everything else is a want. But that doesn't mean we shouldn't indulge in desires from time to time (life would be boring if we couldn't). It is what I'm trying to tell you. Choose your wants consciously, and do not let their constant pursuit jeopardize your financial security. It's not going to be worth it at the end of the day, trust me.

Differentiate between Assets and Liabilities

Just in case you're having a hard time drawing a line of distinction, here's a simple definition: Assets are valuable things that belong to you. Your car, house, and savings account are assets. Liabilities are simply debts. Student loans are an example. Now that you've known the difference, I'm trying to convey the message that you should try your best to accumulate assets and reduce liabilities.

Live Within Your Means

Drawing up a solid budget (one that you must stick to) and not living above gives you automatic freedom from the frustrating cycle of working, overspending, servicing debt, and working some more—such a hard way to live a life, I guess. But you can make life easy by learning to live within your means.

Do you know what's better? Living below your means. This is because spending less than you earn leaves you with a surplus — the vital capital that funds your future. It works like magic; you have to try it, ladies; you have to!

Don't Invest in Anything You Don't Understand

For anyone to succeed in an investing venture, it will take critical thinking, discipline, and consistency over time. It is not advisable to take shortcuts, and investing in overly complex products you don't understand will most likely cause a big blow to your long-term gains and capital. Stick with what you know, young woman; a lot is happening in the financial markets now, from Crypto to NFTs and a lot more. If you're yet to understand those, there's no need to invest in them. Don't be carried away by the crowd; most people don't know what they're doing, and you black woman must be different from them. If you're interested, you must learn extensively about them before investing your money in such ventures. Strive to learn more every day, and don't be spooked by cyclical fluctuations in the market.

Settle Debts With the Highest Interest Rate First

If you cannot avoid consumer debt, you've got to apply strategic wisdom in how you pay it off. Simply paying off high-interest balances first exposes you to fewer interest charges over time.

Prepare for Emergencies

Stack up to six to eight months' net income in an emergency fund. It's a simple but effective way to cushion the effects of unforeseen circumstances like a reduction, poor health, unexpected household expenses, and other life events that could threaten your family's purse.

And then, to wrap things up, you must remember that in making preparations for the unexpected, you also have to include proper estate planning. Guarding your assets and providing for your family is often ignored as a golden rule of smart personal finance. If you're yet to make a will, add it to your to-do list and make sure to do that!

Educate Yourself

It'll be reasonable to conclude this segment with this information, wouldn't it? I guess so. You see, many personal finance books are out in the open. I wish this stuff were taught in every high school and college, but it isn't, unfortunately. So you have to prepare yourself. Besides, no one will care more about your money decisions than you. Invest in yourself! It's the best investment you can make. In the long run, the benefits will materialize if you're severe enough.

Oh, beautiful women! I wish I could go on and on because I enjoy the ride. But the coach's going to have to stop here.

I want to let you know that you're capable of achieving anything you set your mind to because you're strong, and your energy never runs out.

I admire your courage and will to outdo yourselves every time. That makes you a black woman, ready to defy all odds and become who you want to be.
I will support you all the way; even if it means me staying up all night typing these words of encouragement, I'm ready to do that to let you know how special you are to me and the world at large.

The world is waiting for your glow! Go on and be Champions, and I'll be at the corner applauding your prowess, smiling like a proud coach.

Go on and win, ladies!

AFFIRMATIONS

1. New income opportunities will come to me
2. My finances will blossom
3. I can rely on my judgments to make sound financial choices.
4. I am wealthy beyond money.

5. My life is rich and full.
6. I will achieve my financial goals.
7. I can change the world for the better with my money
8. I am allowed to be successful and be happy
9. I'm going to use my money to do good to myself and the people I love
10. I can be comfortable with cash when I manage it well.
11. I am smart with my money.
12. It's enjoyable to spend responsibly.
13. I'm capable of saving money to ensure my financial freedom.
14. I won't be a hindrance to leading a financially secure life.
15. I believe in myself making intelligent financial decisions.
16. I can overcome my spending impulses.
17. Spending money responsibly makes me happy
18. I deserve and expect financial freedom
19. I am capable of building and completing a financial foundation.
20. I receive financial success.

21. My finances don't scare me; I have a plan
22. I can always find the positives in my money issues
23. My income can exceed my expenses
24. Hard work will bring me money
25. I can have fun in a frugal way
26. I will be grateful to myself in the future for saving money
27. It gives me joy when I spend money wisely
28. I spend money on what matters to me
29. I enjoy saving my money
30. Generational wealth is always a possibility and within reach.
31. I lead a financially stable life.
32. Wealth knows me by name.
33. I forgive myself for all the times I worked against my financial stability.
34. I embrace wealth for myself and my generation.
35. I am worthy of a high income.
36. I have all it takes to earn the salary I desire.
37. I attract all that I deserve.
38. I do not drown in lack.
39. I am wealthy.

40. I do not accept substandard treatment for my excellence.
41. I love what I do, and I do it well.

KEY POINTS

1. Financial literacy is a crucial step to financial freedom
2. Never live above your means; try as much as possible to live below it.
3. Accumulate assets and let go of liabilities
4. Never stop saving
5. Investing in yourself is the best.

CHAPTER SEVEN

THE CAREER WOMAN

"Every great dream begins with a dreamer. Always remember, you have the strength, the patience, and the passion for reaching for the stars to change the world."
-Harriet Tubman

You probably must have been wondering why I didn't treat this earlier. Do you know why? I'll tell you the truth; I honestly do not understand why as well, ladies. I'll concede.

When I conclude this book, and I, unfortunately, discover that I forgot to add this topic, I'll be mad at myself and make adjustments.

Because a career is something that no woman should neglect, and it's rather sad that many women want to settle for less in their husbands' homes, doing the laundry, the dishes, changing the diapers, you know... and all the other stuff homemakers do. Now I'm not saying that a woman should do these things! That's not my point. My point is that some women want to do these things every day for the rest of their lives!

Not to sound overly ambitious, but you ladies shouldn't have to settle for that! That's straight-up demeaning! And it's what you want? Be honest and don't let life's circumstances define your ambitions; that's your job! So you have to take it on!

It hurts to see women settling for the bare minimum and depending wholly on their partners for support of various kinds. Not to sound rude, but there's no dignity in that for me.

You all are go-getters! Not hiding under the wings of someone else's ambitions! That's unacceptable to me.
Or you probably come from a wealthy home and don't see the need to be hardworking because you have everything you want and need on your back and call? Are you kidding me? Don't you know what it took for your parents to get to that point? Or let's assume you don't know and you only

138

heard stories.

But then how about when you become a Mommy? That should hit, I guess.

You may have the money to give them a better life, probably because your parents left a fortune, but how will they look up to you? What are they going to see in their mommy that will inspire them?

This is why this topic is important! Any form of mediocrity shouldn't be tolerated in your space. You can be whatever you want, black beauty, your skin emulates toughness, and go through whatever you need to get to where you are!

You've got this lady! It would be best if you trusted me by now because we've come a long way together, and I'll need you to do that when I say again that I got your back till the very end.

Now let's start with the momentum we have built. It always feels good to be a source of empowerment to people.

Let's go!

WHAT DOES A CAREER ENTAIL?

There are a lot of ways to put it. But I'd like to have it this way, personally;

It is that path you want to follow for the rest of your life while searching for opportunities to improve and benefit more as time goes by. Now, this is not what you need to do because you need the money or something of that sort; this is what you want to do and excel in!

A career is mainly driven by love and passion for a particular path, and that's why it's pretty different from a job. (We'd treat that as soon as we can as we progress)

For example, one can choose to play football as their career, may not earn immediately from the start, but finds ways to improve themselves while wanting to benefit from it as well. That's a career path. Not one that you immediately gain from for gaining sake, but once you find peace in what you enjoy doing all the time, the word is passion! That's a career.

How about art? We see music, dance, poetry, drawing, painting, and the rest. And then the sciences! Medicine, Engineering, man! There's so much to say, and the list is inexhaustible!

That is what a career path means to me, and nothing has and will change. You should also always remember that it's not about what you're capable of doing; it's about how you feel about doing that thing. That's what matters the most. Do you find peace, enjoy it, and want to improve? So many questions to determine what a career entails. We'll go into details much later about that, but then there's something I need you to be clear about.

Look out.

A JOB AND A CAREER

These words are helpful interchangeably, and it's one of the things that honestly annoy me. Although related, these are two completely different things that shouldn't be used together to mean the same thing. That's an absolute blunder in its entirety!

A job differs from a career by miles on end, and we'll find out why. But let me first define what a job is.

A job can be defined as a duty a person is expected or obliged to do; a piece of work and more like a specific activity which is carried out as part of the routine of one's occupation or for an agreed price which will be paid at the end of an agreed specified time.

So while we ask how a job and a career differ, certain areas should be examined to dissect the distinction.
We're only going to discuss a few, so here we go.

Requirements

The requirements of both concepts can help distinguish between them. There's this form of specialized training and education that a person is required to acquire as he chases his career. And also, there's so much individual energy put into pursuing a job, like having to do a series of personal research to add more knowledge to what you may already naturally have; that's what passion drives you to do.

Want to know better so that you can do better? That's one aspect of chasing a career. Is it a music career you want to pursue? Apart from probably having the natural talent for music, there's still a lot of work to do to be up there where you wish to be. And that's one of the things chasing a career entails.

However, on the other hand, having a job requires less. Since it's not your passion, it's not something you want to go all out. You're okay if you're doing what needs to be done at that point. You're content. Not ruling out that you can also be hardworking in your job, but the hunger to strive for more isn't there. It's the means to an end, so do the bare minimum, and that's all.

Time

Time is crucial in all our dealings in life, and if we're yet to realize that, we have a long way to go.
Chasing a career path is a long-term thing. This is what you want to do for the rest of your life, so even the word "long term" may not be an adequate

qualification.

I wish I could use "eternal term," but that would be too extreme.

No one puts so much work into something to stick around for 2 to 3 years and then vanish into thin air. That'll be a complete waste of passion and the resources you used to fuel that passion.

So yeah, while chasing your career, you must aim for longevity. Well, in my opinion, everything is dependent on each other. Your longevity depends on the hard work you put in. Because all things are equal, your output is determined by the input, and when the latter is poor, we can't expect much from the former.

Some people have worked so hard in pursuing their careers that even in death, their legacy remains. That's what I'm talking about when I say longevity. So many people don't even have to die before their legacy is erased, and the online time they're remembered is when they finally give up the ghost, and soon enough, we hear nothing from them ever again.

They're so many people who have achieved this feat. I love Michael Jackson, and I think he is one person whose legacy will remain for quite a long time. You can add to the list if you want, but I guess you know what I mean now.

On the other hand, the timespan for a job shouldn't be one to last long. I don't know if I've said this before, but a job is the means to an end, which means the short term. But it is not always so. So many people have resorted to working at a job all the days of their lives whether they love what they're doing or not.

They want to get by, and that can be hurtful not being able to do what you wish to due to circumstances beyond your control. But is that it? Are you sure you can't take control of what you want to do?

That's a question I'd keep asking.

Income

Lastly, I'm going to talk about income. Your income as a career person goes far beyond money. There are a lot of other benefits accrued to a person when he is a top figure in his career. They include fame, recognition, respect, and legacy; it goes on and on. These are the benefits of having a fantastic job.

On the other hand, jobs do not provide many benefits other than money at the end of the day. Don't get this all wrong; there are massively paying jobs, but you don't get much more than money.

But we must understand, however, that a relationship also exists between these two things. That they're different doesn't mean they don't have some connection. They do.

A person usually has several jobs at their disposal in their career, and it is generally easier to switch jobs in the same field of work that defines one's career.

However, changing careers is more complex and may require the person to start at the bottom of the ladder in the new job. And that is one rare thing to do, I must say. Have multiple passions for multiple careers? Superhuman!

CAREER DEVELOPMENT

Everything worth trying requires development and improvement. The word career doesn't fully exist without the word development added to it. For as long as a person's career is needed long-term, there must always arise a need for development. If there isn't, you're going to be left behind.

Career development involves a series of activities which is aimed at the overall improvement of a person's career. It usually consists in creating new goals regularly and acquiring the necessary skill set to bring those goals to actualization.

It is directly linked to an individual's growth and satisfaction, which pushes them to acquire the knowledge and skills required for the option or career path they have chosen. In addition, after receiving the desired know-how, he has to put them into practice to achieve the goals and targets he has set for himself.

THE STAGES OF CAREER DEVELOPMENT

The number of career development steps varies according to different writers and thinkers. Some say there are four, some say five, and some say six. Well, I'd stick to five because I think it's good to be in between and whether you realize it or not, you'll always have to go through these steps of career development.

Self-Assessment

This is the first step in career development. I'd say it involves two different situations. First, the individual may consciously assess himself on the kind of career and growth they wish to have; on the other hand, it may happen somewhat unconsciously. That's where we see natural gifts and talents coming into play. People find themselves doing something and find out they're good at it. But one thing that's common between the two is that they're both going to require development. Be it a natural talent or a result of self-assessment. Talent without hard work will not do so much as hard work without talent will.

Career Awareness

The second stage of career development involves exploring the various career paths that align with the self-assessment of the talent you've discovered in the first stage. As I earlier mentioned, there's always more to a career, leaving you with options to pick from, picking the one that suits you best after assessing yourself.

For example, another issue arises after thoroughly assessing yourself and you conclude that you want to become a lawyer.

What aspect of the law am I looking to major in? Criminal Law, Commercial Law, Land Law, the list is inexhaustible, but you have to make sure you look at everything thoroughly so that you don't make a mistake to toe the wrong path that may likely land you somewhere you'd regret.

Goal-Setting

I'd say this is a very crucial stage in career development. The most important event is the stage where one clearly defines short-term and long-term goals for actualizing the career one aspires to. Both short-term and long-term goals need to be limited to start with.

Short-term goals need to be done as quickly as possible, while long-term goals can be tweaked and changed as time goes by.

Skill Training

After serving the career and the goals, one needs to acquire the right skills to ensure growth materializes. This can either take personal training or join a structured training program online or offline. These skills have to be acquired to prevent mediocrity as it is the least expected of a career chaser. Once the right skills are developed, one can begin the final stage.

Performing

This is the last stage of career development; the actual performance. After gaining all the proper knowledge and the necessary skills, the critical part is to carry out the tasks and jobs in the career success to grow in the career path.

You need to understand that the five stages of career development do not necessarily need to be followed in the order in which they have appeared here. They're all part of an ongoing process, and even when one has gotten to the last stage, they will always need to revisit the previous steps to get the proper career growth.

These stages are mostly followed unconsciously by people, and that's not supposed to be an issue. As long as career growth is taking place, everything is in place.

FACTORS INFLUENCING CAREER DEVELOPMENT

Career development is affected by several factors and the way they interact with each other. These factors need to be studied to know what career would suit you and what job will not.

Let's have a look.

Personal Characteristics

Your type of personality, interests, and values (especially work-related) all have a role to play in one's career development. Close attention must be paid to these traits while choosing a career because these traits hardly ever leave, and once a mistake is made, it becomes tough to cope. A thorough self-assessment will, however, help you learn about your characteristics and then allow you to find careers that are just the perfect match for you.

Physical and Mental Abilities

It is obvious that some people are a better fit for some careers than others, and this is because of their physical and mental abilities and limitations. Don't you ever overlook the importance of finding an occupation that will make the best use possible of your abilities?

Socio-Economic Factors

Socio-economic factors can be a hindrance to the development of one's career. For example, your financial circumstances may threaten to keep you from attending college, which may be necessary to pursue a particular job you have chosen. On the brighter side, several ways have been dedicated to overcoming these barriers, such as limited financial resources, namely student loans, financial aid, and scholarships.

Chance Factors

These are life events that we have little or no control over. These events can play a significant role in influencing the careers that we choose and how we progress in them. An example could be the need to support a family which is financially keeping you from pursuing an advanced education to develop your career further. You don't have to blame yourself for issues of this manner because they're beyond your control, and there's no need to worry about something beyond your control because there is nothing you can do about it.

IMPROVING YOUR CAREER DEVELOPMENT

The world is evolving, and the evolution is massive and rapid, and you cannot afford to be on the wrong side of everything because you will be left behind, definitely and by miles as well, if you don't want to evolve with it.

Whatever career you find yourself in, you must always find ways to improve to ensure you are always on top of your game. Having enough passion for driving you crazy and craving more would be best.

I have some of these tips for improvement that I'd love to share with you all, and I'm pretty positive they'll be of help.

Here they are;

Learn Everyday

There is getting better at what we already know, and then there's learning new stuff. But whatever the case may be, make sure you understand every day. Learning may come as a challenge; for example, if you're working on a project and you come across some new information that may be vital to your project but you have little or no knowledge about, rather than chicken out, accept the challenge and strive to know more about it. You never know when you will need that piece of information again.

Be Indispensable

You have to strive to be someone they can't do without. Your value increases when you have complete control over what you can do in the career path that you have chosen. You can achieve this through challenging yourself, learning about new things every day, becoming well-grounded in what you already know, and that entire sort. It will help you stand out from the crowd and be invaluable wherever you find yourself.

Interaction

There should always be a need to engage with people on the same career path, primarily those far above you. Always be willing to learn from those you think will make a great addition to your life. This is a mistake some people make. They let their emotions get the nest of them and choose to be envious of the person they should be learning from. I promise you that doing that wouldn't take you further than you already are.

On the other hand, you must also be willing to share information with people. Always be open to advising people who come to you for advice. You never know where an opportunity will arise from these little chit-chats.

So engage! Interact!

Figure out your Weaknesses

Career development requires you to be willing to improve every day. Find out what you stink at and your weak point, and correct yourself when you receive negative feedback. Except you don't have the passion for whatever career path, you're on, which makes you not fit for it.

Constantly fix up yourself where you have observed that there is a loophole, and with time, you'll become what you could have never imagined.

Be Yourself, Always

You cannot be another person and succeed in your career development. The moment you start pretending to be what you're not, you start losing the authenticity which makes you who you indeed are. You begin to lose your brand to someone else and trust me, that'll be the beginning of the end for you.
Life is a movie; it always plays you.

POSITIVE CAREER AFFIRMATIONS

1. My career is mine alone, and I'll create it.
2. I'm always open to new opportunities
3. I work excellently well; others can testify.

4. People enjoy working with me
5. I don't know it all; I will ask for help when needed.
6. When people come to me for help, I will help them
7. Learning never ends; I will continue to learn.
8. Bring on any challenge! I'm all for it.
9. I will work hard to get what I want.
10. I set goals, and I achieve them
11. A lot of people can't do without me.
12. I will encounter problems, and I will turn them into experiences
13. I make mistakes that I'll certainly learn from.
14. There's so much to be done that I will start working on them
15. Nothing is going to hold me back!
16. I'm going to be nothing but myself
17. I'm going to live my dreams!
18. People may think I'm crazy; I don't mind anyway; I am.
19. I'm grateful to be where I have reached so far
20. I am looking forward to and working towards a better future.
21. I am creative and competent

22. I do not take my work ethic for granted
23. I am confident in my skills and abilities
24. I have to offer something that the rest of the world can't.
25. I am fully responsible for my career success and will take the credit for it
26. I am capable of achieving the impossible
27. I find so much joy in pursuing my career, and it shows all over
28. I have the skills and talents to compete in whatever field I find myself
29. I get closer to where I want to be every day
30. I will always feel the support around me rather than the negativity.
31. I will build my career excellently.
32. I will reach the apex of my career.
33. I am the best at what I do.
34. I achieve my career goals with ease and elegance.
35. I am not deterred by the challenges I face in my career.
36. I pursue and achieve excellence with ease.

KEY POINTS

1. It would help if you did not allow yourself to settle for whatever comes at you.
2. Accept challenges
3. Your career is yours, don't give it to someone else
4. Learning is crucial to career development
5. Always have an eye on your goals.

CHAPTER EIGHT

THE WOMAN LEADER

"If your actions create a legacy that inspires others to dream more, learn more, do more, and become more, then, you are an excellent leader."
—Dolly Parton

She can become anything she has made up her mind to be. She is not held within the confines of where society wants her to be. She can be a lawyer, a surgeon, a pilot, or an engineer, and she can also be a leader.

Gone are the days when we couldn't see this happen, or even when we did, it was too strange to believe. Big ups to the individuals who have worked tirelessly to pave the way for women to rise to the task, to take on anything that arose before them, and own up to their realities rather than shying away from the world because of what it says.

It's a beautiful sight to behold, and the many who feel triggered by seeing women spread their wings need to be checked for sure. Because as long as you have worked so hard to achieve a specific goal, I see absolutely no reason why it should be denied of you because you're a woman. That's just all shades of unfair. And life is already unfair; let's not make it hard for people who try.

People who have proven themselves have to be recognized! Male or female! So it's refreshing to see women doing excellently well in their various endeavors, and that's including leadership.
So shall we?

WHO IS A LEADER?

Defining a leader from the surface perspective, I would say a leader is a person who directs a particular set of people, which could be in the form of an organization, a business enterprise, a religious group, and so on.

But the word "direct" is where the true definition of a leader lies, and it is more than just a single definition. In short, being a leader encompasses so many qualities and attributes. Most of which one must fulfill to be regarded as a true leader.

As we progress, I will be talking about some of these characteristics and qualities, but before then, I'd give a more precise definition than the one I shared previously.

A leader is a person who has a social influence on others and maximizes their efforts towards actualizing a particular goal. I think that's a more comprehensive definition, or don't you think so?

Well, if you still need clarity, there's more to come as we will be discussing a leader's characteristics right away.

QUALITIES OF A LEADER

A Sense of Purpose

If a person who is acclaimed to be a leader has no sense of purpose, then one might want to question the credibility of his leadership. Because who is a leader without a goal? If a leader lacks purpose, where are they leading the followers too? I wouldn't even know. As human beings, if we're not constantly seeing enough reasons why we're undertaking a specific task, there's a tendency that we will derail soon enough.

That is why a leader needs to have a sense of purpose, to incorporate it into his followers' minds constantly.

It helps make the day-to-day process more purposeful, which in turn helps sustain team motivation and personal investment in more significant goals. A leader without a sense of purpose cannot achieve this and shouldn't even be leading in the first place unless he makes improvements.

Empathy

I have observed that most people see leaders as unapproachable and inaccessible. It immensely saddens me because it is what we see today which has been implanted in the minds of the general public.

A leader is far from that. A leader should not just be accessible; he must be able to empathize with their team members. It spurs them up to go out of their way to ensure they carry out their responsibilities diligently and do so without grudges.

By listening to their subordinates and being open about their appreciation for their teams, a sense of value is imparted to the group by the leaders. When people feel valued, it makes them happy, and they tend to do more of what they have appreciated. When leaders prioritize empathy and acknowledge their team members' efforts, they can empower team members to see the vision for themselves and work hard toward its achievement.

Leaders, putting themselves in the position of their team members with a sense of understanding, also help to address critical concerns of the subordinates and provide solutions.

Vision

There's always a bigger picture to be seen behind every goal. This vision makes it almost impossible for a short-sighted person to be a leader.

Leaders should be able to see the bigger picture and forge unity with their team members behind their vision. By incorporating team strengths and core values, a leader inspires their team with the results at the tail end that resonate with individual values and prompt action.

The vision has to be, however, aligned with the organization's core values, or else the work channeled towards the organization's progress may fall shy. One doesn't just have to stay afloat; there should be progress. Without progress, little or nothing is achieved at the end of the day, and with all the energy channeled in the wrong direction, progress may not be achieved.

Creativity

As a leader, you have to be creative and innovative in tackling whatever problems may arise in the course of your leadership. You may have devised a particular way of solving problems but sticking to the status quo for a long time is risky. Times are changing, and the world is evolving rapidly. There is always a need to revolve with it, even taking risks.

You might want to play it safe by sticking to the good old days when there were many new things to be done. You don't realize that the competition is fierce, and you must be as bright as possible to beat your peers.

That won't be healthy for you and your subordinates, who may try their best but get frustrated because they see little or no results.

Motivation

Leaders ought to be good motivators and create goals that align with the organization's values to inspire team members to work toward the company's vision. Coupled with reaching out consistently, leaders empower their team members to work passionately beyond their responsibilities to achieve a common objective.

I must say this. Motivation is not all about inspiring words; you can motivate

167

your subordinates by listening to whatever question they have and whatever idea they have to bring to the table. It gives your followers a sense of belonging and incorporates a sense of leadership in them.

Making Room for Improvement

As a leader, you should never stop trying to find a better version of yourself daily. Aiming for growth, leaders continuously look for opportunities to make improvements for themselves and their teams. This leaning towards personal gain means leaders should always seek feedback and value ideas that favor effectiveness and progress instead of trying to defend their egos.

When leaders create an enabling environment for feedback that isn't just helpful but highly valued, it is a source of inspiration for team members to speak their thoughts and bring the best ideas to the table. This can bring about higher innovation, leading to long-term success.

Communication

I'd speak on this lastly.

A leader who doesn't communicate with us is no leader at all. Because they wouldn't be able to do much of what we've previously spoken about.
Good leaders must be able to communicate with their followers in a way that feels genuine. This does not mean it's a must to be an extrovert or a leader. Many great leaders have identified themselves as introverts! Instead, it means exhibiting empathy, as we discussed before, engaging in active listening, and building meaningful working relationships with those around you, whether they are a peer or a direct report.

Out of so many, these are the few qualities one must possess to be considered a leader. It's so much more than giving orders and overseeing the activities of an organization.

There are several misconceptions about leadership I would like to bring to your knowledge—just a few before we move on.

I'd like to name this topic;

LEADERSHIP MISCONCEPTIONS

We will discuss under this topic what leadership is not to enable you to make your distinctions.

Let's move on.

First of all, leadership had nothing to do with age. Many people make this mistake, and it's high time it stopped.

I need you to rule out such expectations from your minds! You might be shocked at the reality, ladies! Not to sound too harsh, but fools grow old too. Attaining a certain age doesn't make you a leader above those who haven't. You may have a certain level of experience, but that doesn't automatically bestow the mantle of leadership on you. If you still think like that, you need to grow up! Wake up to reality! The administration has not and will never be based on age.

Leadership has nothing to do with your position in an organization. It doesn't matter what hierarchy you are in in your

170

organization; if you're not a leader, that position will not grant you leadership. Let's get that into our heads now.

Too many people talk about an organization's leadership and reference the senior-most executives in the organization. The plain truth is, they are nothing more than that, senior executives and not leaders. When you reach a certain level in your company, leadership is not automatically bestowed on you. Maybe you can find your feet as a leader there, but there are no guarantees.

Thirdly, leadership has nothing to do with titles. I know many things about leadership, and one thing I'm a hundred percent sure of is that leadership is not about what name you're called.

You can be a leader in your place of worship, your neighborhood, and your family without a title.

And finally, leadership has nothing to do with personal attributes or characteristics. I don't want this to sound strange to you. Many people have often associated personality traits with leadership, but I'm here to tell you that it doesn't play so much a role.

Think of a leader, and so many minds trace to an authoritative figure who loves giving orders and ensures they're carried out or an extroverted personality like I earlier mentioned.

No! That's not what leadership entails.

Extroverted charismatic traits are not needed to practice leadership. And those with charisma don't automatically become leaders.

WOMEN IN LEADERSHIP

Now that we've spoken at length about what leadership is about from the general perspective, how about we be a little more exact?

Women in Leadership roles. What does this prospect bring to the table? One might ask.

I want to start by stating that there are always two sides to everything—the advantageous and the disadvantageous.

But you ladies should know me by now; I'm here to blow your horns! For all I care, you're the best and nothing but the best, so all I've got to say about you is the excellent part: even in your imperfections, you're perfect!

So back to the question of the moment.

What does the prospect of women in leadership bring to the table? In other words, why should women lead? What leadership qualities do they naturally possess that can make them a good pick for the team? It's going to be a long stretch; I hope you stick with me through the ride.

Value for Balance

What I mean by balance here is the one between work and life. Or I'd say, Work-Life balance for short. I think women tend to understand better that there is a life outside the organization they are in control of, so it wouldn't be much of a problem when they're approached by, let's say, a subordinate, making a personal request other than work-life. The understanding women often possess for work-life balance places them on a different level in leadership, making it more enjoyable to be led by them.

They are More Empathetic

One of the qualities of leadership we discussed earlier is empathy, and it is common knowledge that when it comes to that, a large percentage of women will be above their male counterparts.

Some people mistake the empathetic nature of women for weakness. They believe that to be a leader, one must be aggressive or assertive. But that's far from the truth, ladies. Don't you ever let anyone tell you that you're wealthy because you choose not to be a dragon?

I'll forever refuse to agree that you cannot be both strong and compassionate. Never!

Great Multitaskers

Women are naturally good at multitasking, and that isn't even a debate. From the onset, everyone should know that. Multitasking is a trait that women possess, and even if just multitasking will never be enough, it counts.

The ability to give decisive and quick responses to simultaneous and different tasks or problems at a time is vital to being a successful leader.

Better Communicators

A more significant percentage of women communicate better. I honestly do not want to make all these sound like a debate, but I can't seem to help it.

Be it communication with employers, co-workers, or partners, women know how to use this tool excellently well. As we've previously discussed, a communication stream allows for clarity in carrying out duties and responsibilities. Female leaders can already communicate regularly, clearly, and openly. And believe it or not, this is a big plus to whatever organization or team they manage.

Flexibility

This quality is often overlooked when it comes to leadership, and it marvels me. Rigidity makes it hard for people to evolve. You'll be left behind because you're too busy still trying out your old-fashioned practices and wondering why things aren't going as smoothly as they used to be.

Anyways, women are more open to new ideas from people and would likely waste no time in implementing those ideas. Especially when they notice that the system they had formerly adopted is no longer working as it used to.

Inclusiveness

I believe that the male and the female gender naturally have different ways of approaching certain things. Wouldn't you agree with me? I guess you would. With our concern being leadership, I'd say that women tend to be more inclusive, they reach out more, and they care a little more.

A necessary attribute to possess as a leader is the ability to carry everyone along. And I think that women have the upper hand on this one.

Emotional Intelligence

Emotional intelligence is the ability to recognize the emotions in yourself and that in others and relate. It's like putting your legs in someone else's shoes to try to understand certain things you would not ordinarily understand. And it is something that has recently gained cognizance as a vital leadership attitude.

I also firmly believe that this comes more naturally to women than men. (Trust me, ladies, I'm trying my best not to make this look like a debate)

But to be honest, I have experienced this several times, so yeah, I'd agree with that. To truly create a great place to work and to get the best out of subordinates, exhibiting emotional intelligence as a leader is crucial and should not be overlooked.

Ability to Handle Crises

Many women, especially mothers, are naturally trained caretakers who know how to deal with crises at home with so much compassion and patience. These qualities are very relevant when a woman leader deals with problems relating to her subordinates.

Defying the Odds

Lastly, women make great leaders because of the circumstances surrounding their ambitions. It's not a piece of new information that the odds are always stacked up against women being in leadership positions. So when you see a woman at the top, you should know that it took more than the average for her to get there. You know when you're the underdog, it's going to take a little more than the norm to get to the top.

The challenges women face and overcome in their journey to leadership make them extraordinarily strong and capable.

They had to fight so hard to get there!

It is no doubt that from the onset, women's leadership has been revolutionary, and they have made a huge impact wherever they find themselves at the top. Well, this is to tell you that you can defy the odds too and become a great black women leader who is proud of her heritage and will put in the necessary work to achieve the best results.

You are extraordinary women who encompass these values and even more and will make great leaders wherever.

I want to let you know that you're killing it wherever you go; you are limitless, full of strength and vigor, capable of being what you want and not what people have said you are.

Never afraid and never relenting, you are the epitome of the woman leader!

POSITIVE AFFIRMATIONS FOR LEADERSHIP

1. I am a natural leader
2. I am proud of my team, and they're also proud of me.

3. I am willing to explore new ideas.
4. I communicate skillfully.
5. People are aware of where they stand with me.
6. People achieve unbelievable heights under my leadership
7. I welcome the opinions of others
8. Challenges energize me.
9. I love to see my team succeed.
10. I have faith in my leadership skills
11. I never stop improving my leadership skills
12. My leadership is flexible
13. I'm an inspiration to my followers
14. I always see the bigger picture
15. I run with a sense of purpose
16. I will always bring out the best in my team
17. I respect my colleagues, and they respect me too
18. Challenges don't and will never deter me
19. I am a leader with knowledge and understanding
20. I feel great when I see my team excel
21. I become a better leader with every passing day.
22. I can handle failure and will forgive myself for the mistakes

23. I judge the situation well and make excellent decisions
24. I am willing to step out of my comfort zone
25. I am a model for my followers to emulate
26. I don't need to prove anything to anyone but myself
27. I am not afraid of taking calculated risks
28. I am confident that teams need leaders like me to move forward
29. It will never happen that I give up on my team
30. I am not going to disappoint all those who believe in my abilities
31. I will not be a partial leader.
32. I embrace quality leadership with the whole of my being.
33. I am not a despotic leader; I lead with wisdom and fairness.
34. My subjects listen to me.
35. I am surrounded by issues that make leadership easy.
36. I was born to be a great leader.
37. My leadership is a blessed one.

KEY POINTS

1. Being a leader is not dependent on age or position

2. Women in leadership are revolutionary
3. Leadership is not only about giving orders
4. A leader should be empathetic
5. One has to strive to be a better leader every day.

CHAPTER NINE

THE BLACK WOMAN AND BEAUTY

"There is no definition of beauty, but when you can see someone's spirit coming through, something unexplainable, that's beautiful to me."
-Liv Tyler

The fact that after having the worst day of one's life, one will still find himself sleeping for hours like the worst didn't just happen is beautiful. What is beauty? Who is beautiful? Who is the beholder?

Whenever the word 'Beauty' is mentioned in any article or gathering, any place at all, the first thing I think about is that it's relative. Oh, yes, beauty is undoubtedly close to physicality. It means that I could find a diastema attractive and a dimple unattractive.

When it comes to the physical attributes of a person, then beauty varies from person to person. But it would be utterly vain if beauty was attributed only to the aesthetics of a person and not what was in their heart, how they behaved and treated others.

This is why whenever I'm talking or writing about the black woman and beauty, I always go both ways, the physical and inner beauty.

Beauty is like art (it is art, in fact); it owes no explanation; experience got nothing on it; knowledge is even let down; consciousness is shifted to the subconscious- one can only be attracted, not by one of the senses(sight) but, all.

The black woman is a woman, a shade of women. Do you know that black is all the colors put together in one? Black possesses all the charm, splendor, spark, and thrill, but it is always considered dark at one glance.

BEAUTY

General Overview of Beauty

We've established that physical beauty is relative. For a general understanding of beauty, you, my dear black woman, should note that beauty has subjective and objective aspects. That is, it can be perceived as subjectively based on the feelings of people, the opinions they hold, or even their tastes, and objective-based on a property of things. The subjective aspect of beauty is why people say, *"Beauty is in the eye of the beholder."* To date, we do not have an account of who the beholder is, so we can trace that generation to be the judge and pass a verdict on who is beautiful. But that is true, but I'll tell you this: the beholder has always been with you from day one, always standing close to you, walking with and begging for your attention all this while. You should know now that the beholder is the person you see when you look at your reflection. Do you appreciate your body, struggles, dreams, and status? Do you look back and look at yourself now and admire just how far you've come?

Black woman! To become beautiful, you must be attracted to yourself first. When you are, the world will see how total you are. To be black means to have survived; it was never easy for you, the world was challenging, and you had to be harsh or more demanding, which is the foundation of your beauty. That means you are strong; look at your skin and smile sometimes *"Hey, rhino, nothing can mar or impel you."*

Check out gold- it takes all that heat to become the sparkly thing we all know, and you know you can't just pick it up quickly; you'll have to spend big. Think that! You're rare, remarkable; you're beautiful without even trying.

BEAUTY; THE INSECURITY

Hey girl, you've been staring at that magazine for quite a while now, and I

186

see that you do that almost every time I walk by your house in the morning and evening. What exactly are you looking at that you cannot just take your eyes off the pieces of paper? Let me have a look. Kim Kardashian, Beyonce, and Rihanna look so beautiful in these magazines. But I just stared at those pictures for a minute, and I already don't see the need to look over and over any longer.

Are you sure you only find them beautiful? Or is there something else to it?

Hello, young lady. Anytime I drop by to visit a friend, you're always tuned to Entertainment News on the TV. Most of the time, I believe they repeat shows, and I must have seen you more than twice, watching the same show. Don't you get bored or something? I'm a little bit concerned, you know. What's going on?

I can tell that these two ladies have passed the stage of admiration as they absorb the contents of the magazine and the screen, respectively.

The look in their eyes. It is no more extended admiration. The eyes have changed, and the excitement has disappeared from their faces like the evening sun setting into the clouds.

They're no longer admiring the stars; they're now disgusted by themselves, and their look is revealed to me.

"She looks so perfect! Look at her eyes, her skin, smooth as the moon! Her perfectly rounded face gave me goosebumps the first time I saw them on TV, but now, I feel so horrible that I could never achieve such a feat." One of them said, *"Can you see how skinny I look? Just take a look at the woman in the magazine! Those curves are a representation of heaven on earth! I want to be like she is! Why have I even created this way? I'm fed up!"*

Beauty insecurity can make a mental mess of most women these days, and I wish I had a magic wand that could bring everything to an end with just one swing.

Because it's not worth it! Most of the time, what they see in magazines and TV shows isn't even real. These people have significantly benefited from make-up artists and surgeons to make them look good, and you're letting them cause unnecessary pain and fuel your insecurities.

That's just too bad, and to make it worse, society has also set standards for beauty, which are having horrible effects on women every day, leading to more horrible consequences, a few of which will be discussed below.

Low Self-Esteem

Every woman who takes these beauty standards to heart and falls short in one way or the other tends to suffer from low self-esteem.

For instance, when society has declared a specific style old-fashioned, many people who have no choice but to stick to those trends will likely suffer low self-esteem any time they walk down the road. They don't want to be scapegoats. They don't want to get home at the end of the day, open up Twitter and see that there are already numerous pictures of them taken unaware, and then they have to be the laughing stock of the day. And nobody even seems to care! Well, I do. I'm one of those who believe that you are beautiful just the way you are. If you feel like trying other ways of improving your physical looks by working out, or something of that sort, it'll only be a matter of choice for such a person and not necessarily because they have low self-esteem.

Overthinking

So many people can stay up late at night, thinking about how their lives have turned out with the kind of body they have and thinking about how their lives could have been if they had the perfect body instead.

Also, people who have been abused because of their appearance are victims of overthinking. And as they think, they begin to ask themselves questions like, why don't I have the body the society wants? They begin to compare themselves with others and start amplifying their imperfections. Overthinking then leads to the following side effect.

Self-Condemnation

Every day you wake up, you're even afraid to look in the mirror because you're not good enough for your eyes to see. And if you stand in the mirror, it is to backlash yourself. And to tell yourself that you look ugly and that there's no redemption for you.
I thought we were supposed to be our number one fan, but now the standards

that society has denied many people that privilege.

Self-Isolation

I think this should follow after self-condemnation. You don't want to be among your peers any more because you feel they don't like you and judge you, which could be false.

You turn down outings and cancel appointments to ensure that you're not seen among your perfect-looking peers because you feel that their appearances will always find a way to accentuate your imperfections. As a result, you could miss out on so many opportunities that may arrive just because you didn't want to come outside because you hate how you look.

What a flimsy excuse that is!

Desperation

Probably fed up with what you're passing through, you decide that you need to change the narrative soon and that you need to do every single thing possible for you to get what you want.

You can even go as far as implanting artificial body parts to make sure you look good and accepted, knowing fully well that these things have side effects and have caused the death of some people in the past; you don't seem to care, you want to look good, and that'll make you happy.

According to society's standards, you look too thin, take weight gain pills, eat unhealthily, excessively, which may turn into an eating disorder, so many things! To make sure you're in the shape society wants you to be. I wish you don't care, but as it stands, I do not have a say.

In addition, most of these activities you carry out to change the structure of your body have massive side effects on the body, and when the side effects start coming in, you are plagued with trying to make things look better, all to no avail. And your life may never be the same.

That's to show how society's standards can endanger the lives of humans if not properly grounded.
So then, how can we be free from whatever bondage society has made for us?

What steps to take to make you feel good about yourself again?

Let's have some;

Exercise Daily

Taking part in exercise routines is a perfect way to get back in good shape and live a healthier lifestyle. This will not only make you look better physically, but it also ensures that your mental health improves. There are so many benefits of breaking a sweat that you'd be silly not to include exercise in your day-to-day activities. The only way to overcome your beauty insecurities is to face the challenges head-on and not be afraid of the little hard work, as that's a small price to pay for salvation.

If you don't feel too good about how your body is right now, you have to take this chance to step up and make the necessary improvements to the areas that disturb you the most.

Skin and Haircare, Manicure, and Pedicure

Especially as a woman, your beauty routine has to include paying attention to your skin, hair, and nails if you want to look and feel your best. These basic things play a massive role in defining your beauty. For example, washing your face regularly and searching for products that help you take care of any blemishes or dry skin will help you feel more confident in your skin. Your hair, too, is golden. You must learn to care for it or even develop a particular routine to ensure it is always kept in check. Care for your hair by going to the salon regularly and getting the ends trimmed to keep them looking ever fresh and pleasant. In addition, you also have to do well too, get your nails done, or, if you can, do them yourself at home and apply fun and fresh color that makes a statement and gives you the confidence boost you need. You'll feel like a new person if you consistently give yourself the attention you deserve in these three beauty areas.

Go Shopping

One reason a person could feel insecure about how they look is due to their wardrobe. By that, I mean what's in it. If what they own is old-fashioned and outdated and they're finding it hard to find anything to wear, then there's a tendency that they could feel frustrated and unattractive.

First, you need to start by cleaning your closet and removing or donating what you no longer need or wear. Afterward, head online or to the stores to select a few new garments and outfits that will make you feel great and comfortable and complement your figure nicely.

As a young lady, I always went through this routine every few months to keep up with the changing seasons and styles. This is very important.

Keep Records

One significant but easy way to get in better tune with yourself and your insecurities is bordered on is to pen it down in a journal so you can tackle them one after the other. It looks basic but tries it, makes a list, and see with your two eyes what's being the source of disturbance to you or your mind so you can take action. Always record what you don't like and then devise a list of possible solutions to get past and work through your insecurities. Trust me; you don't want to find yourself constantly complaining about what bothers you and then going ahead and doing nothing about it. That's just a waste of paper and pen ink. Always make sure to use your journal as a reality check and write down all you love about yourself and why you're beautiful.

Share with Others

Now, this doesn't mean calling others for their pity, as there's absolutely nothing wrong with opening up to others, especially your friends, about your beauty insecurities and seeking some advice from the outside. You may never know; someone may have suggestions that will significantly help you or allow you to observe your imperfections from a whole new point of view. Search for a trusted friend, family member, or therapist in whom you can confide and who will be willing to listen and give some feedback and advice to you if you're receptive to it. You may find that many others struggle with some of the same insecurities and that you're not alone on this journey.

To conclude, let us not forget that no one's perfect, so you don't have to be either. You will always dislike that part of your body as much as others. However, you have to be open to overcome these insecurities and appreciate what you have going for you that you love. It is all about building your confidence and getting comfortable in your skin. Don't give up until you reach a point where you're able to walk around with your head held high, queen!

Black Beauty

In the past, society did a lot to trample upon black women and women in general, setting high standards to what it meant to be beautiful, and being black was not among them. If you were chubby, had a physical defect, with kinky hair, or the like, you weren't fit to be called beautiful. Over the years, black women have begun to stand on their feet and say, "guess what, we are the ones with our bodies, and we get to decide if it's beautiful or not, not anyone, not even society!"

Oh yes, that's the spirit I see in every black woman I come across, the radiance, the self-confidence reeking like perfume from around them; it gladdens my heart so much that I cannot help but support this cause.
Blackness is more than just one thing; it's not a monolith where you talk about a single skin tone, hair textures, facial features, or the like. It encompasses multiple skin tones, hair textures, and beauty rituals. Black people are taking back their places in retail spaces and beauty brands. I love to see black women sharing their definitions of beauty as opposed to what the society they come from thinks about them. No one knows you better than you know yourself, so I don't expect you to believe some propaganda a group of people brews up against you when you see

within yourself that it isn't true.

This section is about black beauty and owning up to it. For you to be considered a black beauty, it's not necessarily about having glowing caramel, olive skin, or even a copious amount of melanin, dear black woman. Black beauty is about confidence in your dark skin, even its flaws. It's walking up shoulder high and saying to those who try to shame you that despite the massive scar on your face, despite the brown skin that seems to set you aside from the whites and blacks, you don't care about any of it, and you're beautiful just as you are.

One of my close friends from Zimbabwe has this attitude I love so much. Her skin is so dark, and she cares so much for it, applies oil and lotions, goes to the spa often, you know, all of that skincare just because she is so in love with her skin tone. Now, I'm not saying you must apply all the lotions in the world before you're sure you love your skin, far from it. To love your skin is to be proud, show it to the world, and forget about your insecurities. Everyone has theirs; take care of your body and skin, and speak positively about your skin. That's all that is required. It's that simple.

I've been reasonable to be with many black women and seized the opportunity to ask what black beauty means to them. Some say it's confident in your roots, being unapologetic despite what your white counterparts may say about you. It has to keep your head up in a society where you have to work thrice as hard to prove yourself because you're black. You know, one thing that makes people, especially the whites, want to bully black women is because they're afraid of who you are, and let them be!

If they choose to hate you because you're black, you must give them no room for breathing space; oh yes, flaunt your beauty and let them know you're not ashamed of your skin. Wear your Afro proudly, fix those extensions, dress in your traditional clothes or in your English wear, whatever you decide to do, I think what should come first is that you feel good about yourself.

I'll conclude once again that black beauty is about how you see yourself and not what people or society says about you. Rather than hate on your skin or go to the extreme to bleach it, embrace it and love it; apply Shea butter, moringa oil, or whatever is great for your skin.

I'm rooting for you, my precious black woman.

POSITIVE AFFIRMATIONS FOR BEAUTY

1. I am beautiful
2. I love myself at every time of the day
3. My imperfections make me unique
4. I accept myself in all my imperfections
5. I don't need a change to feel attractive to myself

6. I am happy and content with how I look.
7. I appreciate my beauty
8. My beauty has to be seen and appreciated
9. I am sexy and gorgeous
10. My natural look is on point
11. My smile radiates my beauty
12. I am beautiful inside out
13. I am the best of my kind
14. I have zero reasons to feel ashamed of my body
15. I love every scar, every wrinkle, every imperfection.
16. Other people's opinion of my body doesn't get to me.
17. I get complimented for my appearance all the time
18. My confidence is top-notch; it makes the difference.
19. I wake up feeling attractive every day
20. I won't give anyone the chance to make me feel bad about myself
21. The happier I am, the more beautiful I will become
22. I have a positive outlook on life and it makes me more attractive
23. I'm smashing sexy in whatever outfit I put on

24. I accept my compliments because I deserve them
25. I will achieve whatever weight loss goals I have set for myself step by step
26. My skin glows like the sun, and I'm super grateful for that
27. My smile is infectious and makes me look more beautiful
28. I am beautiful inside-out
29. I am in love with every part of my body
30. I radiate beauty from the inside.
31. Every piece of me is beautiful.

KEY POINTS

1. Beauty goes beyond physical appearance
2. Beauty never goes out of style
3. Social media is the perpetrator of harmful beauty standards
4. Insecure people set beauty standards
5. Everyone is beautiful in their way.

CHAPTER TEN

A HEALTHY MIND

"No food will ever hurt you as much as an unhealthy mind"
-Brittany Burgunder

What do you think of when you come across a title like this? Or, what does it mean for a person to have a healthy mind? Take a few seconds to think about the question I just asked and try to answer it.

Time's up! What did you find?

You might have to answer that yourself, but I'm the kind of person who always wants to believe that no one should be wrong about their own opinion. I'm more concerned with giving my two cents and hopping out as if nothing happened.

Yup! That's how I like it.

So whatever your answer was, I guess you were right about it. But give me a chance to say what I think it should be.

I'm going to try my best to try not to impose any of my opinions on anyone; it might be hard, but trust me when I say I'm going to try my best, and if in any way you feel like I'm doing that, I apologize in advance, because one can get carried away sometimes you know.

So I'm begging your pardon from the beginning, and it'll mean a lot to me if you'd remember.

Alright! Let's not waste too much time and get down to the day's business. A healthy mind, let's discuss.

THE HUMAN MIND

Before we talk about a healthy mind, it's fair to talk about the general reason and what it does. Talking about what the mind is and does isn't what should be discussed separately. I mean, talking about what the mind is saying, what it does or is responsible for. So, I won't dwell here for a long time. We do it quickly, and we move as soon as we can!

As we already know, the mind is responsible for many things going on and on in our heads. What have we? Sensation, thinking, reasoning, perception, memory, belief, motivation, desire, emotion, and confidence. Even more, I think, I can't seem to find my way around some more, but I'm sure that there's more than the mind takes care of.

I'm already finding a way to place so much importance on the subject from the beginning. I need to lay the foundation now; look at all the things I mentioned above that the mind is responsible for. They're many, and they are all critical. I have to treat all of them with care. Maybe I'm going too fast already, so I should slow down.

THE MIND IS DISSECTED

We've got three types of minds. This
may sound strange, and yes, it did sound
strange the first time I heard it, but I got
used to it when I finally understood
what it meant, and I believe you will too
when I explain further.

When we talk about the mind, note that
there are three significant concepts to
consider deeply. These include; the
conscious, subconscious, and
unconscious minds.

 It's something we should all be familiar
with, in one way or the other. We may
not see it from the same perspective, but
it doesn't matter much; honestly, it's
good enough that I've got a platform to
share a bit of my mind with you all,
which means, like, the whole world to
me.

To begin, the conscious mind of any
human being is the part of the mind that
we are most knowledgeable about. It is

the part of the mind we use in reasoning. It can be influenced more quickly than other parts of the mind. And what this means is that anyone can change their minds when presented with a compelling argument outweighing theirs.

Please don't mistake the above for vulnerability, though; it doesn't make you less of a human. It makes you more human to be easily convinced sometimes. What if you're wrong about something? Do you see? Your mind isn't always right about a particular thing and may require some convincing.

So when I say the conscious mind is easy to manipulate, don't mistake the assertion for weakness.

The conscious mind is that part of the mind you use in everyday activities. When people bring up "the mind" in conversations, most times, what they are referring to is the conscious part of it.

Next, I'll be discussing the unconscious mind. The subconscious mind is a very active part of the mind, but it is not one that you'd notice very clearly if you're not meticulous. It is the part of the mind that sees everything your conscious mind ignores, from random pieces of information to things that happened in your childhood. It picks up different selections of information and stores distant memories. Then, it brings them to your remembrance on days you do not expect.

Lastly, I'll talk about the subconscious. (Reason why I saved it for the last, I guess you didn't have to wait much longer to understand.) The subconscious mind is the most complicated and, for this discussion, the most important. It is where mental programs are formulated and carried out. If you need to change the way you think so severely, the subconscious mind is where you'll need to focus more.

There's more to be spoken about here, it's exciting, and it's something I'd love to share with you all, but I'm going to try my best not to dwell so much on it; you might get bored. So after a simple illustration, I'll be done with this.

Let's throw life back to the days we were kids for a bit.
As an adult reading this, this may sound a bit absurd, but maybe later, take a little time to analyze the illustration, and you'll see what I'm saying.

So, as I was saying, as kids or babies, we tend to find a line of relationship between particular things subconsciously. The resulting relationships drawn are solely based on experiences, and experiences differ, so what I'm trying to say in essence is that, for the same thing, backgrounds may be different, and this makes whatever relationship drawn from them differ as well.

Let's use an example, two kids who grew up in different neighborhoods. One of them lives near a pet house where dogs are all nice and squishy, and the other, an environment chokehold by crimes hence, the need for security dogs all over the place. We all know these dogs have no business with being all cute and squishy like the former. These dogs are trained to attack at the slightest knowledge of unusual activity by unusual people.

So this is how it probably starts.

The kid in the friendlier environment first hears dogs barking, and the first reaction is shocking. After that, he tries to find out where the sound had come from and discovers that it had come from a pet dog in his home. At that moment, to the kid, the only thing that can make such a sound is the harmless, strange-looking, furry, four-legged creature always running around the house, and that's what he thinks till he hears the same sound, while the dog in his place is asleep. Oh wow! How's this possible? He'd probably think to himself, but the time will come when he accepts that his furry friend isn't the only dog around. By then, he would have wholly associated the sound with the face he saw.

And then one more thing, the most important, is how his mind reacts when he hears the barking.

Since dogs don't harm people in the neighborhood, the barking he hears is not a call for alarm and could be for anything else, probably announcing its arrival or just anything else but a call for alarm.

On the other hand, I wouldn't have to explain so much. It's all the same logic but just a different environment with a different breed of dogs. And instead of seeing a cute little creature wagging its tail when the kid hears barking, it's a different scenario here in the hood.

The kid would most likely see a ferocious-looking creature with bloodshot eyes running after a person or, in a worse situation, the creature pouncing on its victim and doing whatever harm it could before it's held back. That's not sweet to see for a kid. And that's where it all starts, especially when this happens almost daily. That kid then grows to ignore the sweet side of "man's best friend" even if he is told in school by his teacher that dogs can be harmless; I don't think words of the mouth can erase the notion he has from what he has seen. It's even worse when a dog himself attacked him.

So you see, that's how the mind works in the subtlest of ways. They're both kids, but the difference in the environment has changed their notion of how they'd see the same thing.

That's why the black woman needs to be very conscious of the environment she raises her kids. I'm talking to you ladies. Even if you didn't have it quite right while growing up, you must make sure you don't make the same mistake your parents made. Black ladies are great mothers! Don't forget that!

And that's that for the subconscious mind. I hope you can see how important it is, relate the illustration with other aspects of life that can affect the mind, and take the right action where you should.

After a fair dissection of the different types of the mind, how they work, and their importance, it's time to move on to something new.

TAKING CONTROL

I have been going through a breakup, betrayal, loss of a loved one, job loss, racism, sexist situations, domestic abuse, man! There are a lot of these issues that can make a mess out of your mind. I'm supposed to talk about these things, but why ponder so much on the problem when there's a solution to be given? I'm making a bit of sense, am I not?

Anyway, while we admit that everyone goes through a lot of stuff that could make their minds a mess, we also have to acknowledge that there are solutions, and you need to do something about them.

Tell me, does it sound weird that you have to control your mind? I'm asking because it may only make sense that our minds hold us instead. These are just two contrasting opinions that may be both valid anyway.

Want to know my take on this? I would be more than delighted to let you all know. That's all I've been doing all this while, so why not?

Well, to me, it goes both ways. Your mind takes control of you, but there's a catch. You've got to take control first. In other words, whatever your mind controls you to do, is a product of

217

whatever has been done to it (life comes at you fast, you know?) I think that makes sense. Or, maybe not yet, but as we go further, I think I should be able to make you understand. And I believe you all trust me to do all that.

So the main question here is how can one control the mind? There are many ways to do that, and we're going to explore quite a number.

Here we go!

Know What You Face

In other words, you've got to identify what thoughts you need to eliminate due to whatever life has brought your way. Maybe your ex broke up with you because he wrongly thought he had found someone more beautiful. (No one's more beautiful than you are, my black queen.)

I know it's hard not to feel that sting of low self-esteem all over the place. Now that's where you should start!

You must know what thoughts you're battling and be sure you know. At first, gaining total control of your mind could be difficult due to damage done. Or, you could be an over thinker with a sense all over the place. But despite all of these, I need you to know that gaining control of your mind is not impossible, and you shouldn't see it as such.

But you have to take the proper steps and put first things first. Taking time to learn and understand specific patterns effectively will help you make the most of other tips in this book.

Acceptance

You've been friends with your best girl since childhood, and you think you can shy away from the pain of her betrayal in a day? Come on! That's impossible!

Though it's human nature to avoid thoughts that cause distress, there are certain things we can't just avoid, and that's life. (It feels like I've said this for the 1000th time now).

I've never seen anyone overcome mental distress by avoiding the thought. So why don't you try the opposite? Ask yourself.

"Damn! I've been playing again, haven't I?" It helps, you don't know. It does!

When you dwell on those mistakes you've made and how it's making you feel, before you know it, solutions start pouring in. It also helps you keep your mind in check because you don't want to make the same mistake again, except you enjoy pain. So ladies, dwell on that pain for a while. It helps.

Switch POVs

This has to do with self-talk.

Talking to yourself during rough times does a great deal in helping to contain the negative vibes your mind tries to spread. But there's something more. Most of us use the first-person perspective during self-talk, which isn't a bad idea at all. But you're also open to other options, you know.

How about trying the third-person perspective? Instead of saying;

"I failed again, and I feel so miserable. I've been through worse, so I can come out of this too." Why not try;

"Hey, baby girl, I know you've done it again, and I know you're feeling all shades of miserable now, but you've done so much to get over worse situations. So this shouldn't be too much of a big deal for you. Level up, girl!"

That changes the mood. I won't lie. It's like you're distancing yourself from a part of you that only feels the distress, with your bright side sitting across the table. Switching your perspective helps trick your mind into seeing yourself as another individual, giving you the distance from your hardships.

Positivity Always!

As regards mental health, this solution will always find a way to surface every issue. Never underrate the importance of staying positive, ladies!

Positive thinking will not automatically redirect whatever dart life throws at you, but it does change how you feel about it. Now I've got to remind you that thinking doesn't mean pretending everything's going well, ignoring problems, or refusing to consider helpful solutions. Not!

Instead, it is restricting your thoughts' negativity and looking out for the brightness in the most grey skies. No matter how grey it is, there is some brightness somewhere. You have to find it by looking carefully, try zeal and hope.

Therapy

Learning to control your mind is not as easy as it may seem. It's beautiful if you feel you cannot do it on your own. Do not hesitate to seek the services of a therapist whenever life overwhelms you. It is not a thing of shame; speaking up and asking for help is a thing of strength and never weakness. Take care of your mental and emotional well-being. It is essential. A therapist will do a great deal in helping you identify underlying issues and explore potential solutions.

Therapy allows you to feel all your feelings, identify them, and heal them gradually. Remember that healing is a gradual process and doesn't happen in one day. Give yourself grace, my black queen.

In conclusion, it is not impossible to gain control of your mind. You don't need psychic powers to control your mind. But it's not an easy thing either. It takes time, but you'll be okay in the end. Again, remember to give yourself grace.

POSITIVE AFFIRMATIONS FOR A HEALTHY MIND

1. I'm mentally stable
2. My mind is healthy
3. I've been through a lot, but I'm standing here still
4. I love myself more every day
5. I'm not going to run away from my problems
6. Instead of negative thoughts, I will think positively
7. Self-care is my priority
8. The challenges of today are the stepping stones for tomorrow
9. I accept that because I can't always influence things beyond my control.
10. Tough times never last; I'll see the end of it.
11. I find peace with who I am now.
12. My mistakes do not define me
13. I will not allow negative vibes to creep all over me

14. I don't know the future, but I'll be forever hopeful.
15. I'm focusing entirely on improving my mental health
16. I am loved
17. I am in control of my mind
18. I will provide the best environment for the mental well-being of my children
19. I'm happy with whatever I am right now; it can only get better.
20. I can do this.
21. My life is filled with positive people and things
22. I am creating better mental health for myself by the day
23. I accept all the positive and negative aspects of my life in good fate
24. I am always at peace with myself
25. As long as I'm alive, my journey never ends. I will keep improving
26. I choose to be happy regardless
27. I am letting go of all my insecurities
28. I will always choose actions that improve my mental health and make me happy

29. My mind cleanses itself from bad energy and negativity
30. My mind holds memories of love and happiness.
31. I see my scars as trophies.
32. Nothing will make me come undone.
33. I have a brilliant mind.

KEY POINTS

1. Environment plays a vital role in shaping the mind
2. There are three types of reasons, the conscious, unconscious, and subconscious
3. Controlling the mind is not an easy thing to do.
4. Always be aware of your mental challenges
5. The functioning of the reason is primarily a result of experience.

CHAPTER ELEVEN

BLACK WOMEN ENTREPRENEURS

"When you're an entrepreneur you have to go in feeling like you're going to be successful."
-Lillian Vernon

Not quite a while since we spoke about black women managing their finances. Now we're here again because money is in the life of everyone and shouldn't be treated lightly.

Although entrepreneurship isn't all about money, we can't be blind to the fact that money plays a role in it, so it should be recognized as one of the integral parts of entrepreneurship. So you've got to pay attention while we go through the in and out of entrepreneurship and how it can be a tool in the hands of the black woman to make life better for herself and those she loves.

So at this point, let's build around the subject until it's deemed full-fledged enough to raise important issues and their probable solutions.

So here goes.

WHO IS AN ENTREPRENEUR?

An entrepreneur is an individual responsible for creating one or more businesses. They can also be accountable for investing in already established enterprises to make profits. Entrepreneurship is the process by which the above is set up, and it involves taking a lot of risks, bearing a lot of losses, and enjoying the profits that proceed.

I feel like it's a bit different to do what I'm about to do, and at the same time, I think it's necessary.

How about we look at a few successful women entrepreneurs who we can look up to for knowledge and motivational purposes? It wouldn't be too bad to read this book and then have to know about some names to speak if you find yourselves when the subject comes up anywhere.

Just brief profiling of their lives, and we'd be done.

GISELLE KNOWLES-CARTER

Popularly known as Beyoncé, the "Halo" crooner is a singer-songwriter born on September 4, 1981; her career in the entertainment industry started in the 1990s as a teenager. Aside from being a successful entrepreneur, she has her name stamped as one of the most influential persons in American Pop Culture, selling millions upon millions of records all over the globe.
She has also signed multi-million-dollar endorsements, has her brand known as Parkwood Entertainment, Beyonce

produces movies and music, and has her clothing line.

Over the years, she has garnered a lot of fame and accolades, which of notable mention include 28 Grammy Awards, 26 MTV Video Music Awards, 24 NAACP Image Awards, 31 Bet Awards, and 17 Soul Train Music Awards, making her one of the most awarded artists of all time!

In 2014, Billboard had her named as the highest-earning black musician of all time, while in 2020, she was included on time's list of 100 women who defined the last century.

I can't find the words to describe the magnitude of such achievements, man! Unbelievable, I must say!

Let's move on.

LYNDA RAE RESNICK

Lynda Rae Resnick is a successful billionaire entrepreneur and philanthropist born in 1943 in Baltimore, Maryland, US. Together with her husband and business partner, Stewart Resnick, they facilitate several companies worthy of mention, including POM Wonderful, Fiji Water, Wonderful Halos, Wonderful Pistachios, and The Telefloral Company through their holding company known as The Wonderful Company. The company currently boasts of annual revenues exceeding 4 billion dollars.

Interesting right? Something to note. She runs the business with her hubby! While that's very sweet if you ask me, many people these days are against women having to do anything with men to assert a certain level of equality or superiority over men. Don't get wrong, I'm not against Feminism as it may seem, but people have a specific idea about it that doesn't resonate with my reasoning. You don't have to treat men as enemies to assert a particular position that society currently clamors for.

I hope society realizes there isn't a need for a gender war. It's very unnecessary.

OPRAH WINFREY

Oprah is a household name worldwide as she is considered the most powerful woman in the entertainment industry and one of its most famous black entrepreneurs. Yeah, she's black, and she's killing it!

Oprah Winfrey, born January 29, 1954, in Mississippi, U.S, is a successful actress, talk show host, philanthropist, entrepreneur, and author. She rose to be where she is from a very humble beginning.
Best known for her talk show, The Oprah Winfrey Show, broadcast from Chicago, which was the highest-rated television program of its kind in history and ran on national TV for a 25-year

period of 1986 to 2011, she was also named the wealthiest African-American of the 20th century, was at a time the only black billionaire on the planet and arguably the greatest black philanthropist in history of the United States. By the year 2007, she was sometimes ranked as the most influential woman in the globe.

I know this information is what everyone knows, but it sounds new every time. A perfect example to black women and women of all racial backgrounds, Winfrey continues to use her success to launch brands and build awareness worldwide.

MADAME C.J. WALKER

She was best known as America's first Black female self-made millionaire, as recorded by the Guinness Book of World Records. A daughter of formerly enslaved people, Walker worked in a barbershop for only $1.50 a day before she created a homemade remedy that helped her hair regrow after suffering a scalp condition.

Born December 23, 1867, Walker made her fortune by developing and marketing a line of cosmetics and hair care products for black women through the business she founded, Madam C. J. Walker Manufacturing Company. She also became known for being a philanthropist and activist. She died on December May 25, 1919.

DANA ELAINE OWENS

If you know her, you'd be aware that she's a model, actress, and musician but do you know she's also an entrepreneur? Well, if you don't, that's a take-home for you.

Nicknamed Queen Latifah, she partly owns Flavor Unit Entertainment, a production company specializing in television, movies, and artist management. She was born in Newark, New Jersey, U.S, on March 18, 1970.

If it were up to me to go on, I wouldn't even be able to exhaust the list of names I've got, and you probably all know. Many black women worldwide are making headlines with prominent figures in dollars, and that one should be inspired.

Have you thought that you can't be more? Has anyone told you can't be more? Have you told yourself you can't be more? Well, maybe you should have a rethink.

I hope you enjoyed your way around some of the few women who have made it big in the entrepreneurial world. Well, I did, too; if you ask me, it's always fun talking about issues like this and inspiring too!

Moving on, we're going to explore a few types of entrepreneurship, and I'd like to break them down into four types.
Let's look at them one after the other;

SMALL BUSINESSES

As the name connotes, these businesses are small and typically don't have any intention of becoming a chain or franchise. Firms like these include restaurants, retail stores, dry cleaners, daycares, and self-employed individuals. Most of the time, people in charge of small businesses make use of their own money to get things started and only make a profit if they are successful in their venture.

SCALABLE STARTUPS

These kinds of businesses attempt to rise quickly and become profitable full-fledged companies. These ventures are less joint than small businesses. However, these startups are more likely to gain a lot of attention when they become successful than small businesses. These are the kinds of companies you hear about, started in an attic, a garage, a dorm room, or a study room on campus, as an idea thrown around by two friends who decided to act on those ideas.

These small-scale concepts may be the talk of the century, gaining investors and enabling them to grow and scale up. Most people think of this when they hear "startup" or "entrepreneur," and they envision companies like Microsoft, Amazon, or Silicon Valley.

INTRAPRENEURSHIP

This type of entrepreneurship usually occurs like a breakout from a more significant and stable establishment. A lot of times, when entrepreneurs work for a larger organization as an employee, there's a possibility that they'd see the potential to kick off new products or services that take on a life of their own. These people we now call intrapreneurs wield an entrepreneurial mindset to use the resources their current employer has made available to them. These people tend to think outside the box and continue to proffer solutions to potential problems for current and future customers. This model allows entrepreneurs to get things up and run, and it's all thanks to the support from a larger establishment.

SOCIAL ENTREPRENEURSHIP

Humans create specific societal issues and sometimes call for creative community-based solutions.

This is where social entrepreneurs take advantage of the situation by trying to create a positive change with their actions. They do this by establishing an initiative or what we call a non-profit organization, whose primary objective is to provide help to people and not make profits; these people strive to be the change they want to see in society, and their activities are centered around topics that focus on racial justice, gender inequality, environmental conservation, or serving abandoned communities in one way or another.

I believe they're other kinds of entrepreneurship, but these are a few that we can all relate to. As you read through, which one of these kinds of entrepreneurship interested you the most? Not everyone will be an entrepreneur in the end, but I don't see why you shouldn't venture into one if you have a passion for it.
Start wherever you can, there's so much to be explored in the world, and you can be part of it if you want to.

WHAT DOES IT TAKE TO BE AN ENTREPRENEUR?

Like I said earlier, not everyone can be an entrepreneur, and some make attempts, but it's hard to say that they unfortunately fail. Yeah, I understand that the passion is there; many people have the power, but when there's a but, it's always pretty hard to navigate the hurdles one will face.

Certain qualities are required to have as a budding entrepreneur to be able to make a name out of their passion.

Here are some qualities you should have as a woman wanting to make a name as an entrepreneur in whatever field you want to venture into.

PASSION

To me, this is the main attribute of an entrepreneur. Without passion, I don't think anything can work out fine. All other qualities exist to fuel that passion you have for a sure thing. Your work has to be your passion. Because you tend to enjoy whatever you're doing and stay highly motivated when you have the power for such. It serves as a driving force, and with that force, you're motivated to do whatever it takes to be better.

It is a passion that enables you to put in those extra hours in your office or deprive yourself of sleep which can or may make a difference. Like I said before, there are hurdles to go through

240

at the start of every entrepreneurial venture or any venture. Even with certain privileges you may have, your passion plays the most significant role in ensuring that you can overcome these hindrances and forge ahead towards your goal.

KNOWLEDGE

Whatever prospect you wish to venture in, knowledge will always play a key role in facilitating its success.
As an entrepreneur, you must possess considerable knowledge of your field of interest. How would you be able to solve specific problems that you would encounter without knowledge? Only with the understanding that a difficulty can be tackled or a crisis resolved.

Knowing enables you to be aware of the developments and the constant changes occurring in the field in which you are based. It could be a new trend in the fashion industry that many fashion enthusiasts are making quite a fortune from or advancement in technology that makes a particular activity in your field of interest easier to navigate. As an entrepreneur, you should keep abreast of such knowledge as you will be left behind while others move forward.

Passion drives you, but knowledge guides you to leave the competition behind. New bits and pieces of information may prove as helpful as a newly devised strategy, and you will most likely be on the wrong side of the tide without being aware of it.

RISK-TAKING

You'll be an average businesswoman if you can't take risks. Why settle for average? The black woman can always do more. I have a lot of faith in you.

The truth is, without the will to venture into the unknown, it is impossible to discover something special and unique. And without a doubt, uniqueness is what makes all the difference if you ask me.

I don't want to sound like risk-taking is an easy job; it involves a lot of things.

Using unorthodox methods is a risk. Investing in ideas nobody believes in, but you are also a risk! It takes a lot of willpower to do such things, but it might be worth it in the end! In addition, entrepreneurs must have a well-calculated approach to risks. Promising entrepreneurs will always be ready to invest their time and money. But, they always have a backup plan for every chance they take if their plan doesn't work out as expected. That's where weighing the odds comes into play.

Evaluation of the risk to be undertaken is essential. A good entrepreneur won't risk it all if he doesn't know the consequences. Never forget.

PLANNING

A school of thought may consider this quality the most important of all steps needed to make a great entrepreneur. I agree with them, but I'll still take my passion for it. However, you still have to recognize that it's difficult for anything to fall into place without planning. You know what they say, "If you fail to plan, you plan to fail." It's that simple. Planning is simply laying out the whole game ahead of time. It is a summation of all the available resources that allows you to devise a framework for how to reach your desired goal.

Then apart from planning, you also have to make maximum use of the resources you've used in planning. Confronting a crisis with a plan will always be better. It provides you with the guidelines with little or no damages to be incurred.

PROFESSIONALISM

It is one quality that's less talked about, to be honest. And that's sad because it is a quality all promising entrepreneurs must possess but sadly, it's always overlooked. An entrepreneur's mannerisms and attitude towards whoever they work with will go a long way in developing their organization's culture.

Alongside the attribute of professionalism is reliability and self-discipline, which plays a vital role in helping an entrepreneur reach their targets; as an entrepreneur, never forget to be organized and set an example for everyone looking up to you.

When you're reliable, it results in many people trusting your ability. For most ventures, trust in the entrepreneur keeps the people he serves locked in and whatever work he has in the organization motivated and willing to put in their best.

Trust me, ladies, professionalism is one of the essential characteristics of an entrepreneur.

I honestly wish I could go on and on because the list is inexhaustible. But I think this is also a proper place to stop, or isn't it? I hope it is for my queens; they mean a lot to me, and I'd let them know whenever I have the opportunity.

Well, I want to draw the curtain close here, there are many more exciting topics to discuss, and I honestly can't wait to share them with you. However, you know I'd never leave you without the affirmations, don't you?

I honestly wish you could feel how I feel having this little talk with you ladies. I feel blessed, and I wish I could do this forever.

That's how much you all mean to me, ladies.

AFFIRMATIONS

1. I attract success
2. I am willing to get to know about new things every day
3. I'm ready to take risks
4. I will always have a backup plan
5. I am creative
6. I'm a boss

7. I've got everything I need to be a successful person
8. I fear nothing
9. I am smart
10. I have a passion for whatever I do
11. I trust in my capabilities
12. My hard work will pay off.
13. I am blessed with unique talents.
14. My voice will be heard
15. I'm not going to give up
16. I can achieve anything without limits
17. I'm not going to doubt myself
18. My challenges make me stronger
19. I turn my failures into stepping stones
20. I own and am in control of my destiny.
21. I created my definition of success; I'm not pressured
22. I have ideas for success overflowing through me
23. Other people's expectations of me do not define my success
24. It is my time to succeed, and that I will do.
25. When hard times come, I go through them patiently.
26. I am proud of myself and what I have achieved

27. I make the best decisions to forge ahead
28. It's not more accessible, I get stronger and better
29. I'm not a failure; I learn and win.
30. I have the power to overcome my challenges.
31. I beat on every side.

KEY POINTS

1. An entrepreneur is responsible for the running of a venture or investing in an already established organization
2. Without passion for an experience, it will most likely fail.
3. There's much more to do apart from having the power, however
4. Entrepreneurship is for everyone.
5. Entrepreneurship is never easy.

CHAPTER TWELVE

SELF-LOVE

"You are what you believe yourself to be."
~Paulo Coelho

I think the concept of 'self-love' is something we're all too familiar with, yet it's not emphasized enough. Hence, I strive to explain what it means and how and why you should practice it as simply and concisely as I can. Chapter two of my book, "Milestones," with the title, "Self-love and The Black Woman," encompassed a lot about self-love and how to love yourself. It's a great book.

Honestly, you should read it sometime.

Before we go into the day's business, I've got a quick story to share, the story of my perfect friend, God rest her soul, and I believe it will help drive the point home about what self-love truly means.

Nancy was a promising young woman who was just about to clock twenty-seven and walk the altar with the man she had always loved all her life when we heard the news that she had committed suicide. It still hurts me today because I knew why, and when she told me about her problems, I had tried my best to make her want to relax from the negative thoughts, but I guess it wasn't enough.

Nancy always complained of being treated wrongly by her fiance, and at one point, it pissed me off because everyone was telling her to quit. He was too toxic, often gas lighting her and playing the manipulative card to the point that she had low-self-esteem, inferiority complex, and self-loathe. I had never seen anyone hate themself as much as Nancy did. Her fiancé, whose name I choose to withhold for? Reasons, made her believe she would never be good enough and that he was only doing her a favor being with her. He downplayed her intelligence and dished spiteful words at her daily.

"I'll never be good enough." Those were Nancy's last words to me before she died, and it shouldn't be a surprise why she said that. Amongst a host of other things, she was being bullied and manipulated adversely; I believe Nancy lacked self-love.

Self-love is a powerful force against people who wish to bring you down. Very powerful. Do you know how it is with those comical characters and their superpowers, like Batman, Superman, and Flash? Yeah, that's how self-love is with humans. It gives you this form of protection, like a coating against any negative thought, and here's an illustration.

Say, for example, you love yourself so much that you believe you can achieve anything you set your mind to, that nobody is allowed to talk down on you, and that you're the only one who can make or mar your life by the decisions you make, it would be hard for someone to come up at you and say you're a nobody. Go back to the quote by Paulo Coelho and reread it. Yes, my beautiful black woman, you are what you believe yourself to be. If you think you're beautiful, then you are. If you say, "Nah, that woman's way more beautiful than me. I've got such a big nose and acne spots all over my face and body, I'll never be able to compete with her," you've got it all wrong. First of all, you're not in a competition with anyone, this is all about you and yourself, and that is one point I need you to carry along as we talk correctly about what self-love means.

WHAT IS SELF-LOVE?

Self-love is a basis for all humans to thrive, and I'd like us to look past the negative aspects of it concerning vanity, pride, and selfishness because that's what comes to most people's minds nowadays. Some would say, "Oh, I love my body, I've got the smoothest skin in the world, and there's nothing anyone can do about it or say to hurt me anymore."

What would happen to you if misfortune comes your way and your skin becomes scalded? I'm not saying you don't love yourself, don't admire yourself. Heck, far from that. I'm saying self-love is beyond your physical attributes, so yes, you can try out all the facial and body care regimens, but within you, you're continuously thinking of how much of a failure you are, whipping yourself in the dark and wishing you had just enough courage to end it all. But what if I told you that it's not courage you lack but self-love? The American Association of Suicidology has stated that the risk of suicide is increased daily by the lack of self-love. So congratulate yourself because you've chosen to push through and not give in to self-loathe.

Remember that courage is the ability to remain strong in the face of adversity, so choosing to stay through it all and hoping for a better future is something brave of which I must commend you!

Self-love involves:

- Accepting yourself fully.
- Treat yourself with utmost kindness and respect.
- Nurturing your daily growth and wellbeing.

One must also be aware that self-love does not only embrace how you treat yourself but also how you think and feel about yourself. So, when you try to understand self-love, you would have to imagine what you would do for yourself, how you would talk to yourself about yourself, and how you would feel about yourself, reflecting love and concern for yourself.

Loving yourself gives you an overall positive view of yourself. It doesn't necessarily mean that you feel positive about yourself every single time; that's just crazy and would be unrealistic!

This is it; for example, there's nothing wrong with temporarily feeling upset, angry, or disappointed in yourself. It happens a lot to me, but that doesn't mean I hate myself. I still love myself, of course!

Don't let this confuse you; however, I'm here to put you through, so I'll ensure you get every bit of information right.

Just think about how things work in your relationships with other people. For example, I love my son even when I feel like locking him up in prison for a week. Even amid my anger and disappointment, my love for him will influence how I relate to him. It enables me to forgive him, look at things from his point of view, consider his feelings, meet his needs, and make decisions that will support his wellbeing. It is how self-love works. It is very much the same. And this means that if you know how to love others, you know how to love yourself! Or it's more like; if you know how to love yourself, you'd know how to love others.

SELF-LOVE VS NARCISSISM

Now, in addition to the fact that people question the necessity of self-love, another loophole in the practice of self-love is that people believe it's narcissistic or selfish. But that's not the case at all.

That's far from the truth, and I'm here to testify.

In encouraging self-love, psychologists and therapists do not mean anyone should put himself on a pedestal above everyone else. The thing with narcissists is that they believe that they're better than everyone else and will never concede or be responsible for their mistakes and flaws. They're also obsessed with seeking overwhelming amounts of validation and recognition from people. Narcissists also lack empathy for others.

On the contrary, self-love has nothing to do with showing off how much of a great person you are; that's just being delusional.

The people who love themselves in the best way are very much aware that they are flawed in their way and make mistakes, and they accept and care about themselves despite their imperfections. Self-love doesn't stop you from extending the arms of care to others; it just means that you can give yourself the same kindness you give to others.

PERFECTIONISM AND ILLS

The Ills of Perfectionism

Unfortunately, most of us in the Western world have been groomed to believe that the "quality" of perfectionism is a great one to have. After all, being overly obsessed with details leads to excellent work and perfect results. And this personality trait gives us something to brag about during job interviews.

Quality? Really? It's appalling that people think perfectionism is a quality or a virtue. But honestly, to me, it's a vice and one of the toxicity components. There's nothing good about perfectionism, nothing at all!

I want to re-emphasize that perfectionism is destructive for you (bad isn't the word). Not just "not ideal" or "harmful when excessive," but actively deficient in its ordinary sense, like doing drugs or being obese.

Now I'd like to let you know something. Are you aware that a shorter lifespan, irritable bowel syndrome, fibromyalgia, eating disorders, depression, and suicidal tendencies are only a few of the adverse health effects of perfectionism?

I don't think you thought it was that serious, but trust me, I don't even advise you to try because it may eat you up before you're aware and can come out of it, and that's a fact, my queen. There's no good side to this one.

Another revelation here; trying to recover from heart disease or cancer is also harder for people under the bandage of perfectionism, which makes the few who survive and the general populace more prone to anxiety and depression afterward.

DEALING WITH PERFECTIONISM

Now that we've established what perfectionism is all about, we don't have to waste too much time before we try to figure out what we can do to move away from perfectionism.

Well, first things first, you have to be humane enough to accept that it's not a good thing for you. Constantly berating yourself over every little error will slowly but surely chop away your sense of self-worth, making you a less happy person, and you need no one to let you know that you deserve better.

Like Kristin Neff, a human development professor at Texas University at Austin, said — "Love, connection, and acceptance are your birthright."

In essence, being happy is what you're entitled to, not something you need to earn or have someone give to you. Even the United Nations adopted a resolution recognizing that the "pursuit of happiness is a fundamental human goal." it's that important, my queens, don't ever let anyone or anything take that sense of self-worth from you. Not your boss, not your friends, not your ex!

Again, you should also try your very best to resist the urge to beat yourself up for beating yourself. Sounds strange? It shouldn't. In simpler terms, you don't need to kill yourself for being a perfectionist in trying to break out from the shackles of perfectionism. That's just doing what you're trying your best not to.

And if you think you're doing yourself a favor, I'm afraid you're only making things worse.

According to Paul Hewitt, a clinical

psychologist in Vancouver, Canada, and author of the book *"Perfectionism: A Relational Approach to Conceptualization, Assessment, and Treatment,"* the inner critic harbored by perfectionists could be the same as *"a nasty adult beating the crap out of a tiny child."*

You'd probably see something like that in reality and be like *"Damn, what sort of monster does that to a child?"*

But then you're unaware that you do that to yourself daily. How ironic. You need to look inward, ladies.
Spending many years grooming this inner bully, you develop an unconscious reflex to always bring yourself down for every minor thing, no matter how ridiculous.
You know, the little things can drive you crazy, from missing a deadline by even just a day to dropping a teaspoon on the floor; one thing is sure, perfectionists will constantly award themselves a hard time over the most unexpected things, so I don't think criticizing yourself for criticizing yourself is very rare. It happens, man, it happens.

Then again, it's possible to start working towards some much-needed self-compassion. You might feel like self-love is a case of *"you either have it, or you don't,"* but the good news is that psychologists have insisted that it is something you can learn.

So you see, there's hope! Don't give up on yourself, because the moment you do, you give up on everything else!

WHY PRACTICE SELF-LOVE?

It's pretty glaring, ladies; if you don't love yourself, who else will you, love? I mean, it's humanly impossible to love others if you don't love yourself. I don't mean to be too harsh when I say that you're going to be a nuisance to whoever you come across or try to have a relationship with if you don't love yourself enough.

That's the central truth because you will think you're trying your best to love, but you discover that it isn't just working out no matter how hard you try.

And then you begin to feel like everyone hates you, but you don't even know why?

There isn't much to talk about the need for self-love. It's glaring!

It's your right to be happy! There are no "10 reasons why you need to love yourself" this is just it right here, ladies; it is a necessity for healthy living.

You've got to wake up every day and always choose to love yourself no matter what!

And that's on, period, ladies!

HOW DO YOU PRACTICE SELF-LOVE?

Quit The Comparisons

I don't think anyone would boldly say that they haven't found themselves comparing themselves with other people. It happens, but you have to stop making it an everyday thing.

Making comparisons is too toxic to do every day because you take the worst parts of your life and compare them to the best interests of someone else. And you're willing to do that to yourself often so much that you make it a habit?

Think again, dear. Think again.

Be Around People You Feel Good With

If you're constantly surrounding yourself with people who make you feel less of yourself, you might want to change your circle for the good of your mental health.

You can't be around people who make you feel good, and then you won't tap from some of that energy, and you can't surround yourself with people who make you think you shouldn't exist and not be affected by their negativity. That's how it works. Jim Rohn said:

"You are the ordinary five people you spend the most time with."

Think about who those people currently are. Do they inspire you and want what's best for you?

Worry Less

If you don't know by now, worry accentuates self-hate.

I'm going to use this example; you took an examination and didn't do well when the results were out. The average human reaction is to feel bad about the situation and then begin to worry. Letting that feeling linger for longer than usual may not be too good for your mental health because when you begin to worry too much about the results, you start beating yourself up for not being up to standard or for not being intelligent enough to pass the exams and that's a breeding ground for self-hate if you'd ask me.

Quit worrying; it doesn't solve any problem.

There's this thing about the worry I learned.

Why are you worried? Is it something that can be done? Please do it!

Is it otherwise?

Then why worry?

Why?

Go Easy on Yourself

You know, sometimes, when you need to love yourself the most, you end up treating yourself like you shouldn't exist. And that's putting salt on the injury. I find it appalling that some people see such a thing as therapeutic. Well, I don't! Some people call it motivation, but to be honest, you're just being crazy if you do that.

I'm not saying that you should strive for self-improvement or not accept that you've done wrong or something of that sort, but after that moment of chastising yourself for a mistake, brace up!

The world isn't waiting for you to finish telling yourself how stupid you are before it continues moving; it doesn't care about you; the only person that can genuinely care about you is you! So why do otherwise?

Go easy on yourself, woman, everyone makes mistakes, and we're expected to learn from them and not sulk over them for eternity.

Make Room for Healthy Habits

I want to ask you all a question.

How do you feel after doing some form of workout, say, jogging around your neighborhood a couple of times?

Well, I don't know about you, but I feel perfect about myself when I do stuff like that. Even when I'm tired, that good feeling overshadows that tiredness to a great extent.

Do you know why? I'll tell you why I think I feel good.

Everyone knows that working out keeps the body healthy, strong, and fit.

Working out makes me feel like I'm taking a step in the right direction to put my health in order, making me feel on top of the world!

I'd be like, yeah, something's going to feel good in my body in a couple of months or years, and that's one of the things that excite me a lot.

Even when it comes as a dare, maybe I was dared by a friend to do twenty or fifty push-ups. When I complete the task, it makes me feel accomplished, and for a moment, I feel like I can take on anything life throws at me.

You don't get that feeling often as an adult, so whatever you need to do to get it, I advise you to do it.

AFFIRMATIONS

1. I love myself
2. I allow myself to heal
3. I'm OK with moving at my own pace
4. I'm grateful for wherever I am in life right now
5. I'm looking forward to the best that is yet to come
6. I'm at peace with myself
7. I will forgive myself
8. I get better every day
9. The world needs me
10. I will always prioritize taking care of myself
11. I deserve everything I dream of.
12. Good things are coming to me
13. I do not feel insecure about myself
14. I am wanted
15. I am strong
16. I am working on being the best version of myself every day
17. What people have to say about me doesn't affect me
18. I will never give up on myself when life gets hard
19. Everything is going to work out for me

20. I will always be kind to myself.
21. I am letting go of whatever I'm worried about.
22. Some things can't change, and I am OK with that.
23. I am in total harmony and balance with life
24. I am learning how to be supportive of my best self
25. All is well in my world; I am calm, happy, and content
26. I will make time for myself every day because I am worth it.
27. I will always appreciate myself and find other things to be grateful for
28. I'm going to stop beating up myself; it doesn't help me
29. I will not be held back by the weight of my regrets
30. I try my best at all times.
31. All my efforts bring good results.
32. I am full of love.

KEY POINTS

1. It's impossible not to love yourself and love others
2. Self-love is different from Narcissism
3. Self-love can be learned

4. Nobody is perfect
5. Mental struggles always have a way of affecting your physical health.

CHAPTER THIRTEEN

MENTAL/EMOTIONAL HEALING

"There is a crack in everything, that's how the light gets in." - Leonard Cohen

Anyone able to read this has, in one way or the other, been mentally and emotionally hurt. Even the most muscular man on earth has been emotionally hurt before.

Come on! You know how stuff like this works, don't you? And I fear that if I start to give examples, it might trigger past sad memories. So I'm just going to assume that you know what I'm talking about and hope my assumption is correct.

However, we're not dwelling too much on the pain but the healing because that's the only way you'll move forward in life. Well yeah.

So let's move on to what we have next.

WHAT IS EMOTIONAL HEALING?

First, you must know that emotional healing is not a one-day thing but a process; it is a process of accepting all the hurtful experiences that life has brought your way and whatever adverse emotional reaction such experiences have triggered. It means mastering the art of coping with the numerous darts thrown our way in the course of living.

It indeed doesn't materialize in a day or two, but when one is emotionally healed, the mental pain which makes life a little bit unbearable to live (as the case may be) does not hold someone back; to a considerable extent, the mental wounds are closed, and there is no significant pain.

And I speak for all of you when I say that the joy of getting over an emotional trauma is second to none. It's like you've been given a second chance at life after being dead for some time. That feeling of relief is undoubtedly worth the number of times you had to cry to bed, skip meals and classes, and shut yourself from the outside world.

WHY EMOTIONAL HEALING?

Is this even supposed to be a question? It amuses me sometimes why one must stress why emotional healing is necessary.

I mean, rather than someone living the rest of his days in the anguish of mental distraught, why not heal and get it over with? It's much better, ladies, or don't you think so? Well, if you don't, I honestly do think so regardless, and I'd wish for you to have a rethink too.

Mental healing teaches us a lot of life lessons on how to cope and adjust to certain life issues. It gives you an insight into emotional reactions resulting from these life struggles, which will, in turn, help you express your feelings in the best way possible.

When you think carefully before acting upon a situation, it'll save you a lot of stress, and you may not even be aware of it.

That's one truth I'll always stand by. That decision you took after thinking critically, even if it might not have gone the exact way you wanted it, would've been worse if you took another impulse decision.

Finding purpose and meaning connects well with others, and then focusing on good things in life happens. And that's as a result of mental healing. It opens your eyes to many things you may have missed while grieving.

EFFECTS OF EMOTIONAL PAIN

Mental hurt is never easy to conceal. There are no physical injuries, broken bones, or spilled blood, but whatever is going on within your broken heart will always find a way to show itself; most times, you wouldn't notice until you sit and think or someone draws it to attention.

These are some of the reactions of a broken heart that needs healing.

Anger

Most of the time, the people who have nothing to do with whatever pain you're facing are the people who are at the receiving end of your anger. Your very close friends, family, or even a passerby could have a taste of that bitterness caused by your ex, maybe, or your boss and co-workers.

And then even people on the Internet who you've never met or seen by accident before! I know a lot of things like this, especially on Twitter.

A person could be sharing their opinion about something on the net, and then someone comes up with a highly bizarre

comment that leaves everyone
wondering if everything is fine at home.

Yeah, that person could need healing,
you know?

Low Self-Esteem

You might often feel like you're not
enough (we're going to be looking at this
next, so stay tuned.)

It could be two things. Maybe you
faulted, maybe did something to offend
a friend, and then whenever you
remember what you did, you feel guilt,
shame, and disbelief in yourself. That's a
tough nut to crack, to be honest, when
you're wrong.

But the other case could be you being
manipulated into thinking that you're
the wrong person. Most issues arise
from toxic relationships where the guy
always wants to make his girl feel like
she's the cause of every one of the fights
they have and may even push her to

break up with him and then blame her for ruining the relationship.

These are two different scenarios, but they trigger the same feeling, and it's hard to let go of guilt sometimes.

Holding Onto Grudges

People who are emotionally damaged find it hard to forgive. And while you may think that's evil behavior to have as a human being, you may never really understand why they're like that or how they turned out that way. Some people have been hurt by people they thought would never hurt them, and that's enough to drive you crazy, man!

It makes it hard for them not to trust or believe in what they say. It's a toxic way of life, but to them, it's their security, so I don't even want to have a say about why they turned out to be like that.

Insomnia

We can't rule out the physical effects of being heartbroken. Even apart from being unable to find sleep, you feel physically tired most of the time because you've been overthinking lately, and it's wearing you up and tearing you apart.

You didn't have a siesta, so why are you finding it hard to go to bed at night? There are so many ways a human can be tortured, but then the deprivation of sleep comes close to the top. One thing again is that you're not even being productive while you're awake. How can you be effective when you can't even think straight?

Sometimes, there could be a particular thing in your mind, maybe the incident where you have hurt, and then again, there could be absolutely nothing in your mind; you're just staring into the blank space with an empty mind, listening to sad songs to heighten the pain.

Imagine being in so much pain that you want to feel it, probably to know what more it can do to you.

That's quite sad; I wouldn't wish that on anyone; that's a horrible way to live.

STAGES OF HEALING

I've said this before, but I'd like to repeat that no human life is free from challenges or crises. The earlier we understand this, the better.

Yeah, no one wants to experience hardships in their lives, but we have to understand that a crisis is a state that initiates a turning point in our lives. Since we cannot avoid it, we must know how to survive and understand the emotional stages we go through to bounce back from dramatic life changes.

I mentioned a few reactions we might have when we're going through trauma. These feelings form part of the healing or adjustment process, which is long and different for each individual.

A person goes through five stages as they shuffle through the healing process. It is important to note that these stages last for different periods and replace each other, or at times coexist and are not the same for every individual.

STAGE ONE: GRIEF AND DENIAL

We all know what grief is, don't we? Well, it is intense mental suffering caused by specific life issues, like the loss of a relationship, loss of a loved one, loss of a job, and so many more we all know.

I'm telling you the truth, no matter how toxic your relationship was with your ex, a sense of loss still exists when you end things. Memories you don't want to let replay in your head, and the thought that you wouldn't be able to get them again makes you sad.

Anyway, before accepting your loss, there's a tendency that you will deny it, and that tendency is very high, I tell you.

You're going to think to yourself,

"I refuse to believe this is happening to me!"

Denial is quite the norm. Humans use it as a defense against painful emotional experiences that they have difficulty stopping.

However, slowly but surely, you will look at your loss and accept it with faith and growing optimism for a better future.

STAGE TWO: ANGER

Anger is what usually follows after the grief and denial stage. This is the stage where we ask whoever is listening why we have to go through what we go through.

Sometimes you might even be surprised at how angry you are about whatever situation got you into a mess and why it had to happen.

For instance, you broke up with your boyfriend some days ago because he cheated on you. You're going to notice that you might be asking yourself specific questions at a point in your life.

"Why did he have to cheat?"

"Why didn't he tell me he wasn't interested in me?"

These questions are expressions of your anger. Sometimes you know it hasn't happened like that, but that's how life chose to happen, and we can't do anything about it.

However, recognizing anger helps you move on to the next stage, which matters.

STAGE THREE: BARGAINING

This is usually a call for a retrace. After dealing with anger for some time, you may want to return to your toxic boss who just served you a sack letter thinking that if you act or talk nicely or "bargains," decisions may be reversed,

283

and you might have a second shot at the job.

For example, you might say, *"I promise I won't rebel against you if you give me another chance at the office."*

While doing that, you're still hoping that things change for the better and your boss stops being a toxic one. But what's the assurance that such will ever happen? That's why I prefer that you let go. But then, it's something we might have to go through as we go through the healing process.

STAGE FOUR: DEPRESSION

This stage is the deadliest of all stages in the healing process. Severe depression could lead to worse irreversible situations like suicide, and once one has been able to come out of this situation, nothing can hold the person back.

You know we talked about anger the other time. That type of anger was easily expressed and was usually directed at the other party causing you the pain.

This time, depression usually takes the form of unexpressed anger turned inward on yourself. At this point, you think you can no longer do anything to make yourself feel better. (This is usually where suicidal tendencies creep in)

Depression also comes with you losing your sense of self-worth. In truth, this is the most challenging stage and makes one feel withdrawn, exhausted, and helpless. You might not be aware, but that feeling of helplessness hits so complexly and differently. Like, you can't do anything to fix your life; that's one of the worst feelings to have as a human being.

By expression, passive anger is transformed into active anger, which allows us to see things objectively.

Depression, however, makes this very hard to achieve.

STAGE FIVE: ACCEPTANCE

It sounds like it, but acceptance is not a happy stage. It is a stage characterized by a feeling of emptiness, as if the pain is gone, the struggle is over, and rest is at hand. At this stage, faith begins to strengthen, and growth follows. Then a new life is within your reach. This is positive about this stage and not even happiness.

A crisis can do a lot for many people, and people fail to realize this. It can be a person's force to break old habits and bring about unprecedented change. Don't try to rush the process; you must allow time to bring healing, and above all, you must be willing to be a healed person.

While healing, identify your own emotional needs and set realistic goals.

Where do you want to be a month from now or a year from now?

These are the five stages of healing. While you go through these stages, you're not aware of the progress, and the realization usually hits when you've healed completely.

Then you can reminisce and pinpoint the various stages of your healing. You'd only look back and smile at them because you've gone through a lot, and you deserve whatever freedom and happiness come after passing through the excruciating pain of healing.

POSITIVE AFFIRMATIONS FOR MENTAL HEALING

1. I'm going to use whatever hurdle life brings my way to be a better person
2. I am willing to forgive myself
3. I accept and learn from the lessons my pain is teaching me
4. I believe that everything in my life is unfolding the way it should

5. I will be kind to myself
6. I am willing to amend whatever lousy behavior I have
7. As I forgive myself, I am ready to forgive others
8. Everything I'm going through is making me stronger, wiser, and a better person overall
9. The love I expect from others, I'm willing to give back
10. I will always permit myself to heal
11. I am responsible for the quality of my relationships
12. Weeping may endure for a night, but joy comes in the morning
13. I will always allow genuine love into my life and be willing to give as well
14. I acknowledge the past and look forward to a better future
15. My body knows how to heal itself, and I won't interrupt its healing process.
16. My past defines my present and future
17. I am aware of the signals my feelings give to me, and I acknowledge them
18. I am letting go of the past; I chose to live now and in the moment

19. I am thriving in my healing journey

20. I see every new day as a day full of hope and happiness.

21. I let go of the past and believe that everything is working for my good

22. I wish myself well every single day

23. I am open to new ways of healing myself

24. I'm at peace with my body, heart, mind, and soul

25. Happy thoughts play a significant role in my healing process

26. Perfect health is a divine right, and I'm claiming it now

27. I let go of any impediments to my perfect healing

28. Every bridge I need to burn, I do so to better my mental health

29. I'm allowed to have evil days. I am human

30. I experience happiness every day.

31. My grief does not engulf me.

32. I forgive myself for all the times I took part in creating my grief.

33. I will come out of my hurt stronger and happier.

34. I have all it takes to heal.

35. I curate my joys.

36. My pain will not last forever.

KEY POINTS

1. The healing process is not a one-day thing
2. Healing without learning will only leave the wounds open
3. The healing stages do not always coincide. Sometimes they even coexist
4. No human has not experienced a crisis
5. A crisis is a state that initiates a turning point in our lives.

CHAPTER FOURTEEN

YOU ARE ENOUGH

"Know your worth! People always act like they're doing more for you than you're doing for them."

-Kanye West

Having spoken to you about so many aspects of your lives, how things work around them, how to make improvements, and the sort, what's a better way to end the whole thing than letting you know you're enough?

No one is perfect, and everyone has their weak points; your toxic partner that always seeks perfection from you is also hopelessly flawed.

There are a few things concerning your behavior that you might want to put in place because of the ones you love, and that's fine; making efforts to improve is always a wonderful sight to behold, but you ought to know when to stop struggling and accept yourself the way that you've come to be because everyone makes mistakes and the people who you love, that you're trying to make adjustments for, if they don't recognize your efforts, then I firmly believe that they're not worth loving. You should focus your energy on loving the people that do appreciate you and will accept and love you for the person that you are.

This topic can be viewed from many angles, but we will be looking at it from the tip of our self-worth this time. In other words, we will focus on your self-worth and your recognition of self-worth. A lot of misfortunes in the life of people are birthed by the lack of recognition of their self-worth.

For example, a lady will choose to stay in a toxic relationship because her toxic partner always wants to make her believe that she's nothing without him and that he's the only flavor or color in her life. Because she doesn't realize that she's important, these words and actions get to her; she believes him and stays with him, enduring all the pain and anguish that comes as a result of being in a toxic relationship, and in the end, it leaves her feeling damaged beyond repair. (She feels damaged beyond repair even if there's always hope for the living to be whole).

It could lead to depression, and then there's a possibility that she wouldn't be able to take it anymore and may decide to take matters into her own hands and end things.

That's quite unfortunate—a sad ending to a probably once happy life because one didn't recognize her self-worth.

One thing I always pray for as I pen these words down is that as you take a good look at this book, you can take something to run with. That'll be my greatest joy, honestly. Know that many people are gaining value from whatever I have to offer.

So let's begin. Where do we start?

WHAT IS SELF-WORTH?

Before we define self-worth, we must understand the relationship between self-esteem and self-worth. If you think they're the same. I'm here to tell you they're not, and I will tell you why.

Self-esteem is what we think, feel and believe about ourselves and then self-worth is recognizing that you're bigger than all of those things.

Don't understand yet? Leave that to me; I'd do the explaining.

As humans, there are many things we feel about ourselves, good or bad. For example, you may realize that you're always a little too tardy anywhere you go. To class, place of work, church, or any special event you've been to. Now you're not denying that you're a person who doesn't keep to time; that's not what self-worth means. You recognize that you're a delinquent, but don't allow it to bring you down anytime you think about it. You believe that you can overcome it as well! That's self-worth in a nutshell, acknowledging that you're not perfect but not allowing your imperfections to get the better of you.

THE NEED FOR SELF-WORTH

Self-worth is a beautiful thing to have. Many benefits are associated with feeling good about yourself and not allowing your imperfections to drag you back.

We're going to discuss a few benefits of having self-worth, and I hope you find a reason to build on your self-worth if you haven't started before now.

Confident Approach to Solving Problems

Lack of self-worth leaves you feeling like you can't come up with some idea that could be helpful to solve specific problems you may come across in life.

Even if you come up with a good idea, you'd always feel like it's not good enough and won't amount to something substantial. You know what's worse, even when you've got some sort of approval from others, you still feel that there's this missing piece you're looking to fill and that you'd never be able to fill it in.

However, when your sense of self-worth is intact, you will feel confident when making decisions. Because you believe in yourself to work out solutions for yourself, things will turn out great! Even if things don't turn out as you expected, you're still not discouraged because you're willing to learn from your mistakes and try some other time again, feeling more confident to do the right thing.

Realistic Expectations

You may think that when I say someone has a sense of self-worth, I mean that such a person thinks they are perfect and can do no wrong. Well, that's not how it works. It's the other way round.

People who value themselves are not so keen on perfection. They do not demand perfection from themselves.

The reason is that the connection with their essential humanity is so intact that they know it isn't a realistic goal for themselves or others to want to be perfect. And as a result, they don't feel threatened or pressured by the fact that they and others will make mistakes or that the world they live in isn't always safe and reliable.

Have Healthier Relationships

You're going to have a more honest and healthier relationship with people when your sense of self-worth is considerably high, and this is because you don't ever feel the need to hide who you are. You know, many people always look to impress, and as a result, they go the extra mile to pretend and hide the kind of person they are because they believe they're not going to be accepted if they show their true selves.

That wouldn't be the case for a person with a sense of self-worth. Such a person would prefer to be known for who he is than pretend to be someone else to get approval that may not add anything to their lives. We all know that a relationship founded on false characters won't last long and wouldn't even be healthy while it lasts.

It goes for romantic and working relationships, friendships, and family relationships. They'd become more honest and healthier when their self-worth is intact.

Resilience

Many people think that you become immune to setbacks when you value yourself. However, that's not the case at all. Instead, a sense of self-worth makes you more resilient to setbacks; that's the word. Resilience!

When you don't think highly of yourself,

the tendency to feel devastated by failures and losses is very high, and those losses may take their toll on you even if they're relatively minor. You may begin to see them as signs that you are a terrible person or a loser.

But things are different when you feel good about yourself; you're never going to feel like an irredeemable failure even after something you've done didn't go as it should. You're not blind to the knowledge that you've failed, but you don't generalize that label to include your identity. You have to deal with bad things and move on when bad things happen to you.

These are a few benefits of valuing yourself, and everyone is valid.

Everyone wants to be confident in making decisions concerning solving problems; nobody wants to feel bad because they're not perfect; being in a healthy relationship is a goal for many people, and indeed, no one wants to feel like a failure because of one setback they had.

If no one told you before, I'm here to tell you that building your self-worth is a game changer and would quickly make the above needs within reach.

HOW TO IMPROVE YOUR SELF-WORTH

Having spoken a bit on the benefits of having a high sense of self-worth, it'll only be fair to discuss how to overcome low self-esteem and develop high self-esteem to become a better person.

There are a lot and a lot of them, but I'm only going to discuss a few with you.

If you're struggling with a low sense of self-worth, I hope you check them out, and trust me, when you put them into practice, there's going to be a difference, and you're going to notice how better life will begin to look.

Identify and Confront your Negative Beliefs

You're losing your sense of self-worth because these negative beliefs are all over your head. You have to notice those thoughts and challenge them as soon as possible.

For example, you might notice yourself having thoughts like:

"I'm not smart enough to pass this test"

"I'll never be good enough for this relationship."

"I've got no friends."

And so many more negative thoughts are constantly ringing in your head.

However, when you notice these thought patterns, look for evidence that contradicts those statements. Then proceed to write down both comments and evidence. Do well to keep looking back at what you've written down to remind yourself that your negative beliefs about yourself are false.

Come to Terms with the Positives

It is just like doing the opposite of what I spoke about earlier. This time, you're affirming the good things you notice about yourself, which is an excellent way to start.

You can also write down those things that you're good at and things that have earned you external compliments and affection. When you start to feel low, look back on those things you've written to remind yourself that there's still a lot of good in you.

When you start, don't write yourself off when falling back to the old negative habits because they're all part of the process. But with consistent effort, you will find yourself doing better with time and building your self-esteem.

Do What You Love

When you do what you love and are passionate about, there's this eternal urge to want to get better by all means possible, and even when you fail at it, you're optimistic that one day you'll get better, so you don't beat yourself up. Instead, you keep on trying to get better.

Well, if it is the other way round, you'd hardly find fulfillment in whatever you do. And when you fail at it, it becomes a bigger problem because you're not so willing to improve, which bullies you into thinking you'll never get better at it.

Even though you can get better at doing things you don't like, why not do what you want and rest easy knowing that you're going after your passion?

Receive Compliments

People think they're being modest when someone compliments them, and they're like:

"Oh! Can you stop? See. I didn't even hit that pitch aesthetically, or I didn't get the painting completely right, or I didn't score as many goals as I should've."

I used to think that way, too, until I understood that it wasn't doing me any good.

When someone compliments your work, you need to stop looking at that work from your perspective; instead, look at that work from the eyes of the person who has complimented you. Please focus on the things they've said you did well in particular and appreciate yourself for that because you can't always be perfect, so there's no need to try to chase it.

So accept the compliments you receive and move with the satisfaction you've impressed someone in your heart.

Address Yourself With Care

You've got to be careful of how you address yourself so that you don't damage your sense of self-worth by speaking, so I'll tell you that you become what you've said.

You can do this by checking how you use the expression *"I am."*

The expression is strong, and you've got to be careful how you use it. Most of the time, some people react to a mistake they've made by insulting themselves.

"Oh! I am such a fool."
"Oh damn! I'm so stupid for trying to do that."

But is that who they are? Not!

Some people say that it makes them feel good when they insult themselves, but I think that's just being delusional. There is no such thing as that; I refuse to believe it!

If at all you should talk down on yourself after making a mistake, you should approach things a different way. Why not talk down on the action or thought rather than yourself? That's a much better way to approach things rather than call yourself names you do not bear.

You could say,

"I didn't do that thing right." Or

"That idea wasn't a good one."

You know, it kind of moves you out of the ridicule and places what your actions were instead.

The whole idea is that you're not what you've done, so there isn't a need to talk down on yourself. Talk down on the mistake instead; it's healthier.

I wish I could go further, but this will be all.

These are just a few, and I hope you all try them and also not be too hard on yourself when you don't get it right sometimes.

POSITIVE AFFIRMATIONS

1. I am enough
2. I don't need to change; I can only get better.
3. No matter how small, I contribute my quota to the world
4. I love myself more and more each passing day
5. I am unique, and I don't need to be someone I'm not for anyone to like me
6. I am talented, creative, and full of crazy ideas.
7. I have confidence in the decisions I make
8. I will not give up on myself.
9. There's good in me, and I will focus on that and not the bad I tend to see in myself
10. I am my best friend
11. I am beautiful regardless of what others have to say about me
12. I believe I have a bright future
13. I will be careful with the words I say about myself
14. I am grateful for who I am
15. I see myself through kind eyes

16. I will not criticize myself before others do
17. I can face every challenge
18. I don't need external validation to know my worth
19. I am in complete control of my emotions
20. I'm thankful for this journey so far
21. I have the power to create everything I want in life
22. I know what I'm worth and will not lessen myself for anyone else
23. I am one of a kind; there is no one like me
24. My existence makes the world a better place
25. I can find whatever I am looking for within me
26. I am worthy of being praised and rewarded for my efforts
27. I am stronger than my struggles
28. I constantly bask in pure and positive energy
29. I am the only one who can determine my self-worth
30. I'm worth it.
31. I trust my ideas and potential.
32. I am the queen of my life.
33. I am enough at every point.

KEY POINTS

1. Self-worth places you above what you think about yourself
2. Perfection is a myth
3. We can't always get it right
4. Self-worth builds confidence
5. There will always be a chance to do better.

Conclusion

Dear black woman! Congratulations on getting to the last page of this book.

I hope these affirmations pull you out of your dark days, I hope you feel happy saying them aloud to yourself too. Always remember that it is what you declare that you become. Now, go all out and be badass and tell yourself the sweetest things while at it.

I love you.

Thank You

You could have picked from dozens of other books, but you picked our bundle of 2 books

Feminine Positive Affirmations for Black Women

So, THANK YOU for getting this book and for making it all the way to the end.

Could you please consider posting a review on Amazon or if you get the Audio version then on Audible?

Posting a positive review is the best and easiest way to support the work of independent authors like me.

Your feedback will help me to keep writing the kind of books that will help you get the results you want.

It can be something short and simple ☺